No Talent Required:
from Paint by Numbers
To Art Instructor

By
Kathleen E. Hebert

Published by:
Kathleen E. Hebert

****

Preface

Thank-you

A special thanks to my trusted and diligent editors, Susan Nest and Judy Tyler.

Thank-you, Susan, for reading my first draft, telling me the book was possible and then providing the final polishing, painstaking edits. You have the patience of a saint, the eyes of an eagle and the determination of an Olympic star. I am amazed you wanted to read through so many drafts of this book. I am so happy you are still my friend.

Thank-you, Judy, for reading my manuscript with your artist's eye and for guiding me through the first rewrites. Your notes and direction kept me focused—which was no easy feat. You had your work cut out for you.

You both kept me on track and guided me in the right direction when I started to run around in circles. You have been my guiding lights from beginning to end. Thank-you, for making this dream possible.

A special thank-you to Jason Matthews for his wonderful books: *How to Make Market and Sell Ebooks All for Free* and *Self Publish to a World of Readers*. Without Jason's guidance my book would not have been possible.

Dedication

I dedicate this book to my teachers, who told me I could—Blair McClosky, King Coffin, Dudty Fletcher, Mr. Foster, Professor 3-D, Liza Steig and Amira Jamal. They taught me to sing, to dance, to paint and to live. To my students—I never stop learning from them and they constantly give me stories to write. To my mother, who should get the credit for setting me on my path as an artist. I don't think that was her intention, but it was the John Nagy drawing set and the paint by number sets she gave me each Christmas that fired a passion in me for drawing and painting. To Betty Edwards for her book, *Drawing on the Right Side of the Brain*, without which I would never have started teaching beginners. And finally to Helen Van Wyk, who is the reason I finally learned how to paint and the reason I am able to teach others to paint.

Table of Contents

Part I
My Journey, My Teachers

Part III
Tools, Tips and Techniques

Introduction

Who is this book for? It's for everyone who wants to learn how to paint, providing he or she has a good foundation in drawing. It's for the rank beginner, who might not get the basics in class. It's for the advanced student, who needs to brush up on the basics or add some basics he or she may have missed during training. It's for anyone looking to learn a new skill.

It Started with a Dream…

Helen Van Wyk, of Rockport, Massachusetts, was my last art teacher. There are moments when someone walks into our lives and the way we look at the world changes forever. The adjectives "gifted" and "talented" were never applied to my artistic abilities and, after a long series of frustrating attempts at art, Helen finally found her way into my life.

The idea of being an artist did not exist in my life because there was no conscious recognition I was an artist—not from any teacher, friend, or family member. Copying comic book characters and playing with paint by number sets didn't seem to qualify me as any kind of an artist, but I loved how I felt when I was ignorantly dabbling away. Over time, things simply fell into place. I followed one artistic path after another, not because I was gifted, but because art was the one place where I felt peaceful and sane. It was something I loved to do and it wasn't necessary for me to be good at it. I somehow ended up at an art college where, even though I was ridiculed for my lack of talent, I began to discover more artistic passions.

Following college, after many years of taking various drawing and painting classes, with the help of a career counselor, I developed a beginning art class for adults like me—people with no experience or talent in art. After a few years, another twist of fate found me teaching a group of my beginning art graduates how to paint. They had survived my beginning art course and were now ready for painting, even though I didn't really know how to paint. This was inconsequential to them. They pushed me into teaching a painting class and then insisted I start watching a painter, Helen Van Wyk, on PBS. They kept insisting I watch her because she was teaching many of the same things I was teaching them. So, I took their advice and began watching Helen Van Wyk's "Welcome to my Studio" series and I was hooked. Everything I had ever wanted to know about painting, Helen was teaching. I videotaped her one-hour show (featuring two lessons) every Saturday morning and then watched the video every day until the following Saturday. One thing led to another and I found myself traveling to Rockport, Massachusetts, to take a class with Helen, on Friday mornings, through the summer of 1993. Because of what Helen was teaching, for the first time in my life, my own painting began to come to life and, as a consequence, my students' art began to come to life as well.

Each week, after returning from Rockport, excited about Helen's class, I would set up a still life for my students that incorporated my Friday lesson.

For the first time in my life, color was making sense. All those important basics I had never learned, even while in college, were now part of the foundation of my painting and my classes. All my questions were being answered by this remarkable woman and I was eager to share her magic with everyone. The bitter part about this was Helen was suffering from cancer. Helen had been undergoing treatment for a while so each class met as if it was the last one. As her students, we were all aware she had cancer and knew her time with us was short. We hung on her every word, read and owned every one of her books and were devoted to watching her series. She had been teaching in Rockport for twenty-five years. I was indeed blessed to be able to take one summer session with her before she died.

Helen passed away from lymphoma in December 1993. We all deeply felt the loss of this last, great, classical painter and teacher. I had many art teachers over the years, but no one could impart a profound painting principle to me quite like Helen. With wit, charm and an endearing sense of humor, Helen made the most difficult of artistic principles make sense. She was, for many, the foremost authority on painting. She gave us the basics and taught us the foundations we would need to execute a painting. We all treated her with the reverence usually reserved for a saint. And we deemed her words of wisdom as holy. Not only was Helen a gifted painter, she was also a gifted teacher and writer. There was something about the way she put words together that made everything come to life. Now, artistic secrets kept only for the gods were given to each of her eager students as one gives a drink of water to a parched and dying soul. Her words, both spoken and written, implanted themselves in my brain and changed my life forever.

Shortly after Helen passed away, I had a dream about her. In the dream I was looking for items for a still life. I was in quite a snit, rummaging around inside a refrigerator, trying to find just the right combination of objects. In waking life I was not confident of my abilities to set up a still life and, in the dream, I became more and more agitated with this thought in the back of my mind. I had pretty much emptied the refrigerator without finding the perfect combination when I heard Helen speak to me. She told me not to worry. She would help me choose what I needed to set up the still life. I understood she would always help me. As soon as she said this I was able, with her guidance, to make the proper choices and immediately felt at peace, with my confidence regained. Then Helen said, "Don't let anyone forget me."

I woke from my dream in a profound state of emotion. The dream had seemed so real. I was so moved that Helen would come to help me. Of course she would always be with me when I painted and when I taught others to paint.

My mother, over the course of many Christmases, gave me the entire series of "Welcome to My Studio." I still watch these videos each week. I am now able to share the series with my students so they may benefit from Helen's wisdom the same way I did. Helen influences everything I do as a painter and a teacher. Through her words, both in her videos and in her books, she gives me the courage to paint and to teach. It is a bit like having an art bible!

Helen would often tell her students the only way to get better was to paint. It's not about talent. It's about courage. It's about taking a risk. It's about learning about you. For those few hours in front of a canvas or piece of drawing paper, the outside world goes away. Our brains focus. The noise stops. We become peaceful, healed and grounded. Helen knew this. Helen never said we couldn't paint. She said by painting we could only get better.

People think they need natural talent. Not true! This is my story about my journey from ignorance to surviving artist to art instructor. I believe this journey has made me a better teacher and a better person. It is a tribute to Helen Van Wyk, the woman who gave me life as a painter. It is a collection of tips and tricks I have learned over the years as a teacher of nonartists on their journey to becoming practicing artists. It is about the basics and doing it the right way—not the easy way. I know Helen is guiding me on my journey. I hope you will enjoy the story and find here the inspiration to follow your own artistic path.

****

Part I
My Journey, My Teachers

Chapter 1: One Artist's Journey
Are We Born Artists?

It is always interesting to me that people think
an artist's life is one of ease and pleasure where
days are spent creating beautiful works of art, where
the paintbrush or pencil is a magic wand from
which art flows effortlessly onto the canvas or
paper. I'm not sure where this myth comes from
because the reality is many of our well-known
artists have histories of profoundly difficult lives,
mental illness, poverty and many commit suicide
when their art is not accepted by society. Maybe
we are born artists, but for most of us, finding our
path in art is full of roadblocks and detours. Many
people struggle for years before they discover they
are artists. Another sad reality for many artists is
not having their brilliance recognized during their
lifetimes. Such was the life of Vincent Van Gogh.

Did Van Gogh start out as an artist? Does
anyone start out as an artist? My feeling is, if you
are not raised with the opportunities to study, if the
materials required to create works of art are not
available, or if you are not surrounded by art then
that gift or talent may never be realized. Modern
society does not accept the arts as legitimate
careers. The arts are considered "hobbies." Many
musicians and artists have "day jobs." Their
families make sure they become dentists or
computer experts—any profession that will provide
a decent living. They do their art on the side. The
world is full of people who long to draw and paint,

but never follow that path because of monetary issues and family pressure.

My artist's life began in the 1950s when the jobs available for women were limited. Women were mothers and wives. College often wasn't deemed necessary because "you are only going to get married and have babies." Vermont was my home and Vermonters tend to be rather practical people. The climate and terrain are severe making survival a primal concern. Art, as I know it today, was nonexistent. School was the focus. But, as I look back, there were many opportunities where self-expression found its way into my day-to-day life.

Kindergarten

Kindergarten will forever be my favorite class. I couldn't wait to get up in the morning and head off to school and my classroom with the orange door. We would cut and paste and paint and sing and model clay and dance. Every class should be like kindergarten.

I can still see the room full of big windows letting in the light and cardboard cutouts on the room-length bulletin board of a choo-choo train. The engine was black, the caboose was red and the remaining cars were the colors of the spectrum— yellow, purple, orange, blue and green. All the furniture, the sink and the shelves were just the right size for five-year-olds. Kindergarten was like a mini vacation from adult land.

There were two kindergarten sessions each day and I attended the morning one. We would start our day with a chore, such as straightening up the coat closet, or watering the class plants. There was an art project, which could be anything from poster painting on an easel, finger painting or working with clay. There was playtime, which included a set of giant cardboard blocks. Our morning was topped off with a snack, a little bottle of milk and a nap while our teacher, Miss Murphy, read to us. Then we went out to the playground if the weather was nice.

Learning was such a joy. School was within walking distance of my home. My mother would have lunch on the table when my class was over. School was cool and I looked forward to it each and every day.

My favorite time at school was when we worked on our art projects. Finger painting was hands-on, but only two colors could be chosen. I often chose opposite colors on the color spectrum, which turned my paintings brown. Miss Murphy knew many things, but perhaps she did not understand some of the basic principles of painting. I, myself, didn't understand the principle until many years later. Clay was therapeutic as we rolled it into ever longer and longer tubes to be used as bird necks, ropes or nests.

But my favorite activity was painting at the child-sized easel with a paintbrush. Even though I loved finger paint and manipulating clay, there was something so magical about holding a giant, long-handled paintbrush glopped with poster paint and applying it to paper hanging on an easel. The paint dripping down the page, the brilliance of the colors, the paint pots encrusted with paint and the way the paint smelled is still vivid in my mind. I would be transported into another place and time when I painted. I was five. The next time I would paint on an easel would be when I was nineteen.

Grammar School

My formal artistic education ended when I entered first grade. During the first week of that year, I looked out the immense, wood frame windows of the old classroom (my grandmother went to this school) and tried desperately not to cry. I attended an eight-year Catholic school and the scary nun-creatures were strict and overworked trying to control their classes of fifty or more students. The school was far from my home. I often felt isolated and alone. The days were long and frightening. There was constant pressure to achieve good grades. There was endless homework, projects and papers to write. Learning became a depressing chore. Most times we were denied a fifteen-minute recess because we had not covered the required subject matter. Creative projects were not high on the school's list of things to teach us. It was a prison to me that would start each September with me feeling fear and foreboding and end each June with joyous relief and exhilaration. I always felt some part of my life was over and the year would be an endless, exhausting, uphill climb.

If we were lucky, one Friday a month, we had an art class for about an hour before the end of the school day. However, if our other lessons were not completed, we lost our art class. This was the 1950s. The three R's were always more important than art or music. Anything was a welcome release from the constant memorizing and reciting. The material was pounded into us. Anxiety was a normal part of every day. These few moments of "art" were heaven. Mostly the projects were about copying what our teacher was doing, simple cutting and pasting. But it was the only time in grammar school, with the exception of when the nuns changed our seats around, which felt fun to me.

Most of us have painful childhood memories associated with our early attempts at art and these memories often keep us from trying art again. I remember an art project we had in third grade. The object was to place a piece of black construction paper we had folded and cut like a paper snowflake, over beautiful blobs of watercolors to simulate a stained glass window. I was so excited I could make this lovely gift for my mother. However, the project didn't quite turn out the way I had hoped.

The project began with the cutout of black paper. That went well. Then the mixing of the watercolors. My colors started off as they should, but as I added more and more color, something strange happened. My paint started to turn black. In a panic I added more color. This only made more black. My panic increased as the class came to an end. My project was a complete disaster. There was no opportunity to try again and there was no beautiful project to give to my mother. The nun took my painting and held it up for all the class to see. "This is what your project should not look like," Sister Joseph said in her usual sarcastic voice. I was so humiliated—I felt like a total failure. Perhaps Sister Joseph could have taken a positive tact and explained to the class the scientific reason why my painting had turned black: This is what happens when you mix all the colors together. It is possible she didn't know. Unfortunately, I believe many children at that time had similar experiences. Another place where art was pushed into the background and the student was made to feel wrong.

Fortunately, my parents managed to procure a 3-foot by 4-foot chalkboard and some old school desks so my sister and I could play school in our cellar. I'm not sure we played school that much because we both hated school. My father hung the large blackboard and we always had an endless supply of chalk and erasers. It was the perfect place for me to practice drawing my two favorite subjects—horses and angels. The size of the blackboard allowed me to draw life-sized figures. There were no models to work from so I made things up as I went along. There was always a drawing of an angel filling our blackboard—with no nose, hands or feet. Those bits were yet to be learned and didn't seem to be necessary. My uncle, who had access to tons of old-fashioned computer paper, with each page attached to the next and little holes punched along the sides, kept us in great supply of drawing paper.

In time, my skill at drawing horses and angels improved. One Christmas, one of my gifts was a John Nagy drawing set. There was a book, drawing pad, charcoal, pencils, squishy eraser, sandpaper pad for tapering the tips of the charcoal and sharpening the pencils, and a paper stomp for shading. I still have some of the pieces—including charcoal and the paper stomp. The drawings were challenging, but completing them when I wasn't doing homework became an obsession. I had never worked with real drawing materials before and the instructions were extremely helpful. There was one drawing of a boxer. I got to use some of the gray-colored chalks in the set and was enchanted by the effect. The representation of light and dark with these chalks was a revelation but, once again, it would be many years before I could put the concepts into practice.

High School

The grueling routine of school continued, but now it was called high school. Never one of the crowd, I buried myself in my studies and music became my new creative outlet. Now that I was older, my mother gave me paint by number sets for Christmas. Each Christmas would bring two new numbered panels, long-handled brushes and fifteen or twenty little pots of paint. It was the process— the feel of the brush, the smell of the paint, setting everything out on a table in our cellar—that enchanted me. I could sit for hours and apply the colors. It was magical to see the painting as it emerged. Hours would pass as I painted in all the yellow and then all the blue, each number in turn. There was something about the scent of the oil and watching the colors all fit together neatly in their numbered spaces. This may have been a good diversion for someone like me with a mild form of Attention Deficit Disorder. Those few moments focusing on those paintings stopped the incessant chatter in my head. There was a sense of peace and working on them gave me the ability to concentrate and focus. The rest of the world disappeared.

At Christmas, my parents would take us to visit my father's family scattered here and there around Burlington, Vermont. Uncle Fred and Aunt Mary-Agnes were particular favorites as we made the rounds. Uncle Fred was an artist. He would bring out his latest painting to show me. I was intrigued by how he knew how to paint without numbers. I don't remember much about his paintings, but he seemed very cool to me because he was the only person in our family who could paint. He always made me feel like we belonged to a special club even though I could never imagine I would someday paint like a real artist.

During my free time (and there wasn't much of that because there was always so much homework to do), I drew on scrap pieces of paper—often during algebra class where my brain would "short out" trying to understand $a + b = c$. My eyes would start to cross at the thought of another boring and confusing concept. I would whip out my latest piece of scrap paper and start another drawing— usually of a horse or my new obsession—female comic book characters. It was exciting to come up with new ideas for dresses and blouses to put on the models I copied. My favorite was Millie the Model by Stan Lee. Betty and Veronica from Archie comics were my next favorites. I would spend hours copying how they stood, different head and eye positions, and their hands and clothes. When in class I would try to draw the characters from my head. No scrap of paper ever went to waste. Whatever side was not used became a space for my next work of art.

Somewhere in all those scraps of paper, some part of me decided to become a fashion designer. There was no money for college, but I had known, since I was six, college would be in my future. Only one college offered a four-year degree in fashion design—Pratt Institute, in Brooklyn, New York. I applied and was accepted just before Christmas of my senior year. It was to change my life forever, but first there was a trip to Europe.

Europe

The Foreign Study League offered affordable trips to Europe for high school students. My mother decided this would be the chance of a lifetime. Based in Salt Lake City, Utah, the program offered extensive study in European culture and history. There was one program sponsored by my high school that would cover five countries in six weeks. This included room and board, traveling between countries, classes, field trips, the flight over and return trip on an ocean liner. For $1,000 tuition, which I earned by babysitting for horrific, monstrous children, I visited Italy, France, Germany, Holland and England.

Each morning of our stay in Europe began with classes to acclimate us to the country we were visiting—its history, its customs, and the do's and don'ts while we were out and about. Then, we would spend the day on field trips with our group leader seeing the sights. Our days started at 6 a.m., and sometimes lasted well into the wee hours of the morning. We didn't miss seeing one church or museum and often we would attend a play or an opera as part of our tour.

Having remained in Vermont my entire eighteen years, I had never been exposed to so much culture, art and architecture. We sat in the ruins of the Baths of Caracalla watching the opera Aida as camels and horses traipsed across the stage; we saw Michelangelo's "Pieta" and his art in the Sistine Chapel, in Rome; we were surrounded by Monet's "Water Lilies," Degas's "Ballerinas" and the pastels of Mary Cassatt, in the Impressionist Museum, in Paris. Everywhere we turned there was another moment of history, another spectacular monument, another exquisite piece of art. It all was more exciting than the textbooks we were forced to read in school.

As my mother believed, this was the trip of a lifetime. In 1969, most Americans never got to travel to Europe. Our counselor, Sister Jean, had a great deal of experience leading eighteen-year-olds through the mystical countries of Europe. Sister Jean expertly guided us through all the sites, churches, ruins and museums. The museums were my first introduction to art (aside from the paint by number sets). We saw enough art in each country to make our eyeballs fall out, but I wanted to see more.

I fell in love with the Impressionists and started to recognize and look for them in each museum we visited. My favorite memory in France was visiting the Impressionist Museum with Sister Jean—just the two of us. I remember sitting in a room all alone with Monet's "Water Lilies" surrounding me on every wall. I was transported, enchanted, soothed and awestruck by these pieces. I had fallen in love. I could hear and smell the water and feel the light as Monet saw it. I was mesmerized. I couldn't explain it—an eighteen-year-old in love with a dead artist.

Then one day while running through the Louvre (I was lost, which is a common condition for me, and was running to catch up to my group), I came to a dead stop at the bottom of a long staircase. As I looked up, there stood the most amazing sight I had ever seen— "The Winged Victory," a huge headless and armless statue with great wings outstretched. My breath stopped, my body was frozen in awe. I couldn't move as I was so struck by the size and beauty of this ancient figure. I was so fortunate to have gotten lost in order to find her. This statue was created around 190 B.C. and is still as magnificent as ever. How could humans produce these amazing sculptures? I had been having many moments similar to this one all through our travels in Europe—little mini-shocks to my sleeping, artistic subconscious as dormant parts of my psyche began to wake up.

I sat with Monet, imagined chariots racing around the Coliseum, marveled at the faces of the "Pieta" and at the ceiling of the Sistine Chapel. But after six weeks of history, art and music, it was time to return to the states and get ready for college.

College—Pratt Institute

No one in my family had ever graduated from college. It was a lifelong dream for me. As much as I hated the confinement of school, I always knew my school days would continue until I graduated from college. Without the benefit of guidance, I applied for the Fashion Design School of Pratt Institute because I loved drawing the fashion models from my comic books and designing clothes for them.

How I heard of Pratt I don't remember. We didn't have the Internet in those days. But somehow information about the school fell into my lap and this was going to be my school. Pratt was, and is, a prestigious art college. I can tell you I did not get in on my artistic talent. Only good grades were needed to be accepted into the Fashion School. Mine, after years of studying until 2 a.m., were very acceptable. No portfolio or proof of any talent was required. How I got into this college was nothing short of a miracle. There was no money to send me to school so I applied for every scholarship, grant and loan available under the Sun. And, because I wasn't interested in going anywhere else, Pratt was the only school to which I applied.

Two weeks after returning from my trip to Europe, I was on my way to Brooklyn, New York. It was a six-hour journey in a car filled with all the items needed for my new life in a dormitory. Brooklyn was not a welcoming place. My dormitory was simply a reconverted apartment house about twenty stories tall. There were no friendly faces greeting me when I entered my room for the first time. My parents were consumed with horror at the thought of leaving me in this awful place. As they left to return to Vermont, it hit me (and my parents) that my former life was now over. Things would never go back to the way they were. It was a bit like jumping off a cliff.

After three days of tears, grief and despair, I entered into the world of Pratt Institute. Here everyone was miles above and ahead of me—educated, talented and self-confident. To everyone there I was the square hick from Vermont—I didn't talk right, didn't dress right, didn't think right. I had a paint by number set. Once, I naively opened up my set of paints so I could "paint" like my roommates, who were art majors. Big mistake. No one tried to hide her look of contempt. I don't think I could have done anything more to provoke such a disgusted reaction from them. Nothing was said, but in my head I heard, "You are too stupid to live." So I closed my little paint set in shame and humiliation. The good news was I was at the bottom of the pond—I could only go up from here.

Life Drawing with Mr. Foster

Art classes were required at Pratt in all majors except for food science. Freshman year was meant to familiarize us with the many art forms available and my first year at Pratt was the most memorable to me. Everything made an impression on me and my memories are full of moments from that year. I was introduced to enough ideas, visions, people and philosophies to last a lifetime. The year was meant to expose us to many kinds of possibilities. It was a time of awakening, of challenges and discovery.

Life Drawing with Mr. Foster was my first drawing class ever. We were going to be drawing nude models. I can't tell you how exciting that sounded to an inhibited, Catholic, eighteen-year-old. I walked into the room on our first day with my humongous, 3-foot-long newsprint pad, my new drawing pencils and my funny-shaped eraser (a memory from my John Nagy days). I set up on one of the easels. My last easel had been in kindergarten. We were required to stand while we drew. The model came in, removed her robe and took her pose. Mr. Foster said, "OK, you have twenty minutes." I got right to work on my 3-foot drawing pad hanging on to the top of it for dear life. Without looking much at our model, I sketched a pathetic 1-inch version of her head. The model's face was posed in three-quarter view. I knew how to draw that from all my years copying from comic books. I did my standard Millie the Model face complete with bowed lips and long, curly eyelashes. I blindly avoided the model's body. I was astonished twenty minutes went by so fast. And here was my drawing pad with a head the size of a quarter right at the top.

Mr. Foster came up behind me and gently said, "No, no, you have to draw the whole thing," as he pointed to the figure of the model. After three hours of class my pages managed to fill up.

Luckily, the two best artists in class, Brenda and
Laura, stood next to me and every so often I would
peek at what they were doing. They drew with
confidence and ease. They stood away from their
easels using their entire arm instead of having their
faces mashed into their drawing paper like me.
They had no problem easily filling their newsprint
pads with perfectly executed sketches. I didn't have
a clue and I was in a room surrounded by people
who had been drawing and taking art classes since
they were children.

Mr. Foster took pity on me. He gently
instructed, gave me confidence and direction. He
was soft-spoken and had a walrus mustache. He
was enthusiastic and encouraging. I responded
enthusiastically to any instruction he gave me. He
never turned his nose up at my abilities, never made
me feel I was stupid and, with his patient guidance,
I eventually was able to complete a decent, but still
clumsy, drawing of the model in front of me. I
would never dream of missing one of Mr. Foster's
classes—they were the highlight of my week.

As an end-of-term project, Mr. Foster assigned
each of us a self-portrait. In my obsessive
enthusiasm I spent three full days and nights doing
a life-sized pastel of myself, which hangs in my
parents' hallway to this day. Exhausted from a lack
of sleep, I managed to deliver the completed portrait
to class. I left before the critique. My fellow
students later told me Mr. Foster spoke of my
artwork in glowing terms. This kind of appreciation
and acknowledgement was new and somewhat
uncomfortable for me, but there was something
about this art stuff that made me want to continue.

In one of my last classes with Mr. Foster, a
most rewarding moment came when I decided to do

a portrait of one of our models. Something about her face intrigued me. Mr. Foster let me draw without interruption. On that day I was sitting in front of the class and had a good view of the model's face. I was now much more savvy and relaxed than the person who first drew a quarter-sized head on a 3-foot sheet of paper. The drawing seemed to flow and I wasn't doing my usual bit of struggling. At the end of her pose, Mr. Foster brought the model over to my easel and showed her the portrait I had drawn. She was so impressed at the likeness she asked if she could have the drawing. Amazement and shock! Oh my! It was like being offered $500. I was so honored by her request I eagerly handed her my treasured portrait even though I was giving away my "masterpiece."

It was obvious to me Mr. Foster was proud of the work I had done. He didn't have to say anything. The fact that he directed the model to my drawing didn't need any words. That simple gesture would stay with me for the rest of my life. Now that I am a teacher, I understand what he was feeling as he watched someone admire the work of his previously inartistic student.

I will be forever grateful to Mr. Foster for opening my eyes—not just to what was in front of me, but to my own hidden abilities. He generated many positive moments for me. He gave me a lifetime of gifts: Growing and learning didn't have to hurt or humiliate; the impossible was possible. Mr. Foster has become one of my favorite teachers. He showed me learning could be fun. This was something I hadn't experienced since kindergarten. It was his method of teaching, his positive guidance and enthusiasm that inspired me to become a teacher much later in my life.

Two-Dimensional (2-D) Class—The Teacher from Hell

My 2-D teacher, however, was the darkness to Mr. Foster's light. She was the second of three teachers from my freshman year at college who would later inspire the development of my own beginning art class. We were required, as freshmen in the fine arts program, to take a 2-D and 3-D art class. 2-D was about working on a flat surface—like a piece of paper—something with height and width, but no depth. 3-D was about working with objects that had a depth dimension—like sculpture.

I have no fond memories of my 2-D teacher. Mrs. 2-D would assign a homework project and at first, I would go back to my dorm room and eagerly attempt my assignment. What I lacked in ability I more than made up for in enthusiasm. For one of my first assignments for this class, because of the encouragement I received in Mr. Foster's life drawing class, I attempted to do a complicated, 3-foot drawing of my roommate, Kris, sitting at her desk working on one of her art projects. I can still see her hunched over in her chair with her feet tucked around the chair legs, concentrating on her homework. Lucky for me she sat that way for a long time. Considering my background and my total lack of drawing ability—it was an amazing feat to have tackled the composition, portraiture and perspective. After many years, I'm still impressed I was able to execute the kind of drawing I did. Mr. Foster's life drawing class had opened new possibilities for me. There was a surge of pride as I worked on the drawing and a sense of hope. I can still see that newsprint drawing in my head. The page was nicely filled and the likeness of my roommate, in profile, was quite remarkable.

I took my masterpiece to 2-D class and the teacher put it up in front of the other students. I was so proud my piece was chosen. I had worked so hard. I was eager to hear what she had to say. Mrs. 2-D began to critique my picture with a smirk on her face. I don't remember her words, but I remember her insinuations. Bit by bit she picked at my work. I felt my stomach cave-in and all the enthusiasm I came in with was replaced by humiliation and despair. She kept picking. There was nothing positive. She looked at me as if she couldn't believe anyone would bring in something so awful. I felt like a wounded animal being systematically disemboweled by raptors. The critique felt more like a sadistic attack. She carefully and methodically pointed out everything that was wrong and then invited the rest of the class to add their own remarks. Needless to say, there were no kind comments. My drawing was a joke. "How could anyone do something like that?" and "Anyone knows that is not the way to do this." And so it went—on and on.

In spite of this humiliating experience, I managed to show up for every class taught by Mrs. 2-D. Each week was another assault on my self-esteem. My homework project for this class would always start the same way. As I sat in my dorm room ready to begin my 2-D homework I knew, before I started, whatever I did would be awful. There was a feeling of being defeated before I began. There was nothing I could do right. I had no idea what I was supposed to be doing. This was the way we were taught at the time. It was Catholic school all over again. Why was ripping someone to shreds the way to teach? There was never any sense of joy or accomplishment or any sense I was learning anything. I was frustrated, angry and convinced I was hopeless. Mrs. 2-D never had anything nice to say about any project I did for the entire semester—with one exception—our last assignment.

After an entire semester of being ridiculed in class I was no longer interested in spending time and energy on Mrs. 2-D's project. In a state of impatience and frustration, I took an old, cardboard shoe box and removed its cover. I poured Elmer's glue into the interior of the box until all its walls were covered and dripping with glue. Next, I dumped some raisin bran cereal onto the glue and mashed it in until every bit of the box interior was covered with cereal. I set the box on one of its long sides with the interior facing me. I bent an old spoon in half and jammed it through the top of my box. The spoon part was hanging into the interior of the box while the handle was protruding at an angle from the top of the box. The glue took about twenty minutes to dry. I can still remember how angry I felt. I was fed up. What was the point? Ready for yet another humiliation, I brought my shoe box project into Mrs. 2-D. She absolutely loved my project! She raved about how magnificent the piece was, how creative, interesting, and brilliant. I was shocked and stunned. I thought I must be in the wrong class. I didn't get it. I still don't get it. Here, finally, was a success and I was unable to feel anything but anger and confusion.

Three-Dimensional (3-D) Class

The third teacher who inspired the development of my own art class was my 3-D teacher. He was much like Mr. Foster—gentle and encouraging. He never made anyone feel stupid and everyone enjoyed showing up for his class. I remember looking forward to his projects and couldn't wait to start them. I loved his critiques and seeing the other students' projects. Professor 3-D had us build an impressive set of cardboard blocks from different colors of poster board. The set included several multi-sided shapes of various colors and sizes. I ended up with a trash bag full of colorful blocks. From our set we were then instructed to build an art form each week for our homework assignment. We could put our forms together with anything available—pins, tape—whatever would keep it from falling apart as we traveled from our dorms across campus.

Once in class, we would sit around tables large enough to accommodate eight students. With a project in the center, Professor 3-D would take each structure and offer his critique. His eyes would sparkle with enthusiasm as he looked over each student's construction. He centered his full concentration on the work. We could feel his excitement as he investigated each piece. 3-D has to work in the round, which means, it has to look good from every angle. When you are developing a sculpture, it has to be turned while you are working on it to make sure it doesn't have a dull, uninteresting side. "If you add just a bit here—it will be perfect," he would say. I never wanted to take my homework projects apart because they were almost perfect. Professor 3-D was always showing us how it could be better—not how awful it was. In his words, there was always hope. There was no humiliation. There was no attack by jackals.

Professor 3-D encouraged us and encouraged us in the way we treated each other. There was no condemnation, but simply always a way to see things differently and make it better. I always left class filled with enthusiasm. He infused all of us with an excitement for learning and experimenting. I didn't get sick before his class. I didn't dread his class. I didn't face his homework with anguish and anger. When I started one of his homework projects I knew it was going to be wonderful. I knew I could do it. I knew I would figure it out. The contrast between Mrs. 2-D and Professor 3-D would later be a powerful motivator when I began teaching.

Painting

I was sketching and using pastels, but I really wanted to paint. I saw my roommates paint and I wanted to try it. It was pretty obvious I was not gifted with talent, but I did have an abundance of enthusiasm. Being at the bottom of the barrel was a good place for me to have been. Everything I did made me better than I was and it was obvious to me I should keep trying. I had done some portraits, I could draw figures and was learning to do fashion sketching. Everyone at Pratt seemed to have already learned those things that were still a mystery to me. I seemed to always be hunting in the dark.

My roommates taught me how to build a canvas from scratch. They gave me a few pointers about what I would need for supplies. I started painting in my room and loved the feel of the paint and the brushes. My self-built canvases were always badly warped, but I didn't care—I was painting! It was like painting in kindergarten again—the feel of the paint, the look of the colors. I couldn't make anything look real, but I loved applying color and shapes. I loved watching my brush make swirls on the canvas. The act of painting filled me with joy. I eagerly waited for the semester when I would have my first elective. I started taking painting classes in 1970 (my sophomore year).

In the old days, painting and art were for the gifted and the gods, not for those of us bound to earth. It is sad I can't remember one painting teacher at Pratt. What makes me even sadder is I can't remember them ever teaching me anything. In many cases, the teacher wasn't even in class. I was given no list of colors, or told what kind of brushes to get. There was no instruction on how to mix colors together. I once showed up for a painting class with a blank canvas. I stood there for two and a half hours and never managed one brushstroke. I was afraid. I didn't know what to do. No one stopped by to help me get started. When I tried to paint a figure, it would come out green. I had no idea how to do perspective. I was lost. But still something in me had to paint. Every so often, in spite of my ignorance, I managed to produce a painting of which I was proud. I didn't know what I was doing, but I had to keep doing it. I was taking baby steps, but each step seemed like a monumental victory for me. The thought I might be able to do this gave me courage.

One of my former roommates recently tried to convince me college was a good place to toughen me up. I went there to learn something. I could have joined the Army if I had wanted to be toughened up. It was a strange world, Brooklyn, New York. I was counting the days when I could

leave that dirty, smelly city and return to Vermont.
I took more and more art classes while I was at
Pratt, but it wasn't my major. I learned I would
have to figure things out for myself. I didn't know
it at the time, but I came away from Pratt with much
more than I ever realized.

****

Chapter 2: Transitions

Earning a Living

One of my great passions was singing. I have been singing since I was three. One day, as we were leaving a cousin's wedding service, I mentioned to my mother I would do anything to be able to sing in the big church. I was fourteen.

My mother was a part-time organist and she arranged for me to sing at another cousin's wedding. This truly was a big church and I was amazed at the voice that came out of my body. Not bad for a first time. A big adrenaline rush gave me a hunger for more singing engagements.

I managed to learn a bit of guitar (an instrument my mother purchased with S and H Green Stamps) and started playing and singing at events at my high school. The guitar went with me to Europe. My fellow travelers and I used every moment of waiting (there was lots of waiting in Europe) to work on our four-part harmonies and repertoire of songs.

I would copy song lyrics from my favorite records into a notebook. Then I would try to figure out the chords on my guitar. That songbook came in handy as we sat waiting for rides, riding on buses for fourteen hours and sitting around in terminals. I must say we were quite good. The music of The Beatles, Bob Dylan, Joan Baez and Joni Mitchell, to name a few, soothed our restless, teenage hearts. By the time I returned from Europe in August 1969, I could perform twenty to thirty songs. I took my songbook and guitar to Pratt to begin my freshman year.

Having finished my first year at Pratt, I needed to earn some money for tuition and room and board. Back home in Vermont for the summer, I was walking along Church Street, the main street in

Burlington, and ran into a high school classmate. We got to talking. He knew I played the guitar and sang. He told me the bar/restaurant we were standing in front of needed an entertainer. Why didn't I go in and audition? So I did. I got the job singing five nights a week for much better money than babysitting. Wow! A job as a singer!!!! I did a solo act. The owner let me work there during my summers off from college.

I had always had a fantasy about being a great singer performing in front of audiences, but it was never like you see in the movies. Besides, I had terrible stage fright, which never got better no matter how much or how long I sang. But, I did love living at night and sometimes wondered if I wasn't a bit of a vampire, sleeping until noon and avoiding the Sun at all costs. This musical detour would be my life for the next ten years. I have enough stories about being a lounge singer to write another book.

By the time I was a junior at Pratt, I realized I had no interest in becoming a fashion designer. I was seeing myself as a singer and I desperately wanted to leave New York. My guidance counselor was part of the fashion department. When he asked me why I got all A's in my art classes, but C's and D's in my fashion classes, I don't think he appreciated hearing I hated fashion design.

If I wanted to change my major to art, I would have to spend another year at Pratt. I had no portfolio, so getting into the art program was unthinkable. When I thought about dropping out of college, everyone advised me to stay in, finish my four years in fashion and get a degree. I continued singing for my supper through my summer vacations, singing in the stairwells at Pratt and occasionally singing in New York. I graduated with a Bachelor of Fine Arts degree in 1973, and headed back to Vermont.

My life always seems to flow from one point to the next. Planning never seems to work. My life just happens to me. I had been singing at the Holiday Inn, in South Burlington, for two years when I met someone who lived in Massachusetts. He also played guitar and sang. He knew some people in Boston and got me a couple auditions. I started singing at the Sheraton Boston, in the lounge on the second floor. I worked there for two years singing and playing my folk songs six nights a week. I found an apartment on Park Drive, in Boston. It was my first apartment with no roommates.

The one (and only) thing I missed after graduating from college was drawing and painting, so I continued to paint on my own. It was a part of my life that gave me so much pleasure and healing. I knew I wasn't very good. I couldn't paint what was put in front of me. I couldn't paint a landscape or a pot of flowers, but none of that ever seemed to matter.

Liza Steig

While I was singing and living in Boston, I took private art classes, in Cambridge, from Liza Steig, ex-wife of the cartoonist William Steig, and Margaret Mead's sister. Liza was living in a lovely, second floor apartment. I wanted desperately to paint, but none of my experience in college had generated much in the way of self-confidence. When I first approached Liza, at the prompting of a friend, she studied the paintings I brought to her. She praised my work and explained about taking private classes. Once a week, I showed up for my afternoon class to Liza's apartment with all my brushes, paints, easel, palette and canvases.

Liza did not allow me to paint anything real—only brushstrokes and colors on the canvas. Liza kept me talking the entire time I painted and punctuated my lessons with her own artist's wisdom. Each week, for two years, I painted two abstract paintings at each session and always returned the following week eager to paint again.

Liza was appalled at the state of my clothes, which were covered in paint, and taught me the art of staying clean while I worked. This was my first "lesson." That meant I could no longer use my jeans as a paint rag. Holding the brush in my mouth was forbidden. I was painting in her home and I was not to muck it up with paint. There should be no paint on her woodwork if I went to use her bathroom. There could be no splatters of paint on her hardwood floors. This was an invaluable lesson to learn. Oil paint gets everywhere, and Liza taught me to keep clean especially since I was painting in her dining room.

Beginners have certain expectations when they draw and paint. They feel the artwork should look a certain way, and should be something they could sell or show their families. This was where I was. The blank canvas terrified me. I could never get started. Because of my limited skill level, I didn't know what to paint or how to go about painting. I was afraid I would be ridiculed for my ignorance. Painting class meant you showed up and pretty much worked on your own. It's interesting to me my first painting teacher at Pratt didn't recognize I was having a hard time.

Because of Liza, I was learning to let go of my fears and expectations and just paint. I was to paint nothing real. I could use any color, any brush I wanted, any shapes and lines I wanted. She would watch and give me pointers about how to do different brushstrokes, and how to be aware I was only using one brushstroke going in one direction.

During every session, after I had painted for ten minutes, Liza instructed me to turn my canvas upside down. I hesitated. Turn it upside down? This was like bending steel with my bare hands. I was painting blotches of paint and already so attached to the painting I was resistant to change it. However, I was there to learn and I turned my canvas upside down. It was an epiphany. Oh my! I could see what I needed to do. With each turn, the turning became easier and easier. It was a great way to see what I was doing from a different vantage point. By turning the canvas to another angle, I was able to see an area of the canvas that needed more color, or more work. It was another lesson in letting go.

Painters can't paint if they are holding on to an idea, or if they become attached to their painting. It is a challenge for a painter to see what is best for the painting. If a color or a shape is wrong or in the wrong place on the canvas, it must be moved. Painters need to be able to adjust, to change. Attachment to a part of the painting is disastrous if the artist can't let go. Things constantly need to be moved and altered. The entire canvas should be worked at the same time so the painting evolves as a whole. Painting and drawing are about relationships. One thing changed on a canvas changes everything around it. By constantly turning the direction of my canvas I was able to let go of my expectations and just paint. It was freeing and fun.

A painter must learn to paint freely. If each stroke is a manifestation of fear and lack of confidence the painting looks dead and restricted, reflecting that fear and lack of confidence. Painting two paintings each week in this carefree style taught me one of the most important lessons of my painting career—I didn't have to be afraid of the canvas. My approach to painting became less inhibited although I still lacked the skills to draw or paint with any sense of capturing a subject. I spent two glorious years with Liza as she patiently removed my fear of painting.

When I came to the end of my time with Liza, I brought in a newspaper clipping featuring a photo of my grandfather. My mother had cut out the clipping from the Burlington Free Press and sent it to me. I desperately wanted to paint this portrait. There was no logic as to why. It was simply something I needed to do. As I look back, I am amazed at how I was not afraid to attack such a complicated subject. Maybe it was just my profound ignorance that kept me going. Liza allowed me to paint this "real" picture. As I painted in Liza's apartment, I became aware of how I was painting. I was relaxed. I was enjoying the discovery of the shapes, colors and spaces.

This was a black-and-white photo so I had to make the colors up as I went along. Mixing color to produce what I actually saw was not one of my strong suits, but I was managing to get a pretty fair likeness of my grandfather. In the newspaper photo he was seated, but the photo only showed him from the waist up. Dressed in his white, sleeveless T-shirt, he was pointing with his left arm, with his

right arm resting along the back of the chair.
Grandpa always wore a red cap and his pipe
dangled from his lips. I had such fun painting that
day. I wasn't aware of time passing. There was no
inner pressure to "get it right." It was a major
breakthrough. My two years with Liza were well-
spent. I finally managed to break the stranglehold
my blank canvas had on me. The fear was gone.

De Cordova Museum School
      Once again I had the urge to move out of the
big city. I found a sweet, two-bedroom apartment,
in Framingham, Massachusetts. My new singing
job was for the 99 Restaurant chain. I continued
singing for another year, but I was tired of watching
people get drunk every night. I was burnt out.
Guitar playing folksingers were no longer in vogue
in the music world. So I was out of a job and
needed to make money to pay the rent.
      I came to the De Cordova Museum School, in
Lincoln, Massachusetts, through the backdoor. I
had worked as an artist's model in life drawing
classes to pay bills while in college. I loved the
work, I was good at it and, when prompted by a
friend to get back into modeling, I contacted a
number of area art schools in Massachusetts. Never
having confidence about how I looked, art modeling
gave me the self-confidence I lacked. One of the
great things about being a model is you get to take
the class and get paid. You can't be drawing or
painting, but you can absorb the information the
teacher imparts. Observing is a fine skill to
develop.
      The De Cordova Museum School was one of
my favorite places to model and King Coffin was
my favorite teacher. He was the preferred teacher at

the school and we seemed to work well together. He also taught in other areas of Massachusetts and I was often requested to model in those classes as well. I think he loved that I had an art background and was interested in everything he taught. King got me excited about painting. After my two years with Liza Steig painting abstracts, I was ready to continue my painting journey.

King talked as he walked around the class, stopping to comment on each work-in-progress. He was always throwing out pearls of wisdom I devoured like candy. It was not in my consciousness to become an art teacher at this point in my life, but I now realize I was learning about teaching from King. He reminded me of my two favorite teachers, Mr. Foster and Professor 3-D, at Pratt, in the way he was always encouraging and positive.

King even suggested I bring a painting to class to show him. I had been taking ballet classes in Cambridge when I lived in Boston. I was developing a series of semi-abstract paintings of ballet dancers. I had one painting of three dancers I brought to show King. I could see he was excited about the painting and I got to hear the words, "If you just move this here a quarter of an inch, it will be perfect." Well, of course, I changed the painting as soon as I got home. I didn't get the chance to be close to perfection very often.

I adored King and looked forward to working and learning from him. I don't think King was the happiest of teachers. Often, his students would ignore his words of wisdom. I was aware many people took his class because he was the most popular teacher. They didn't necessarily want to do what he said—they were more interested in the prestige of being in his class. I saw him get frustrated with this. He wondered aloud to me why he wasn't home painting instead of teaching. King gave me so much as an artist and teacher. I couldn't understand why everyone wasn't hanging on his every word. What he gave to me worked. I didn't see any reason to question him or ignore him.

Eventually, I was able to afford classes at the De Cordova Museum School and studied with King for a few semesters. He taught drawing and painting. It was a real breakthrough for me to finally have the courage to be taking a real art class, with a real art teacher, at a museum school. King brought the same enthusiasm and energy to his class that Mr. Foster and Professor 3-D brought to their classes at Pratt. He taught me to see the rhythms of an artwork—how one thing connects to another in a kind of a dance.

I taught myself to not press too hard on the paper with my pencil or charcoal. Holes in the paper were not a pretty sight. I was still struggling with the concept of foreshortening. Foreshortening is the visual shortening of something (an arm or a leg on a model as the object comes toward you). You can't see the entire object so you have to shorten it to make it look real. Our brains tend to draw what they know, not what they see, so foreshortening is a challenge in seeing. This was something with which I struggled. I finally concentrated on trying to see and understand foreshortening. I started to put the pieces together. Something changed in the way I was seeing things. In drawing and painting, an artist is always trying to convert three-dimensional reality onto the two-dimensional surface of a canvas or drawing pad.

There is no going in and out on a piece of paper or canvas. You can only draw up, down or sideways.

King passed away when he was sixty-five. He had just retired with the intention of painting and, within a couple of months, had a heart attack. Everyone was devastated by the loss. There was no one with his character, his bristly moustache, his dry sense of humor. I can still hear his voice. I can still see him as he walked around the classroom stopping at each easel to offer advice and support. King had a profound influence on me. He became my mentor without his knowing it. I so regret not being able to share my teaching stories with him. I think he would have been pleased to know he was such a major influence in my life.

At the De Cordova, I then studied with Dudty Fletcher for a couple of years. I still had no clue I would soon be teaching an art class. I remember sitting behind a lovely woman each week over a period of time and thinking to myself her work never changed. It was not really good or bad, but it never seemed to go anywhere. I made a mental note to never allow my students to remain stagnant if I was ever to become a teacher. My inner teacher was taking notes!

At some point in Dudty's class, she introduced a new and exciting book, *Drawing on the Right Side of the Brain* by Betty Edwards. It was some newfangled approach to drawing and I was stubbornly set on resisting any attempts to try something different. It was now the 1980s and I had been doing the same thing (badly) since 1969. I was comfortable with my struggle and resented anything rocking my boat. Dudty had us copy a drawing of Igor Stravinsky by Pablo Picasso upside down.

As I began the exercise, drawing in this weird way, I was consumed with anger. A voice in my head kept saying "This isn't the way to draw." I found myself stuck about a quarter of the way down the page. Since the drawing I was copying was upside down, I did not have a clue what I was drawing. I was furiously trying to draw what my brain was screaming at me— "the leg, the leg, the leg." I finished the drawing and when I turned it around, I was dumbfounded. The drawing was perfectly executed and "the leg" I was trying to draw was actually a part of Stravinsky's suit coat— not a leg at all. The entire class had experienced the same thing.

This book, unbeknownst to me, was a turning point in my journey as an artist because it would become the basis of the art classes I would eventually teach. It was a revolutionary concept that anyone could be taught to draw. And, it would begin to fill in many of the key points of drawing I had been unable to understand. Immediately, I went out and bought a copy of the book.

A New Look at Teaching

Because of Liza, King and Dudty I began to develop self-confidence in my abilities as a painter. And, to save my voice when I was singing in Boston, I found Blair McClosky, a well-known voice therapist. He gave me a voice I could always count on; a voice with power (something I would need as a teacher).

These four people were teaching me how to teach. They did not make me feel bad. They did not humiliate me. They infused me with their passion. They helped me to see and to hear and to use my voice. They encouraged my growth and corrected my mistakes in a way that made me want to learn more. How fortunate I was to find them. They will always be my heroes, my mentors, and my guiding lights. I can't imagine what my life would have been like without them.

****

Chapter 3: Becoming a Teacher
In My Thirties

In my thirties, I began cleaning houses for a living. There was something very grounding about walking into chaos and putting things into order. Never good with finances, I now had steady jobs and money I could count on each week. I continued taking art classes at the DeCordova and on occasion would attempt a painting on my own in my little apartment in Framingham.

After several years as a one-woman cleaning service, I found myself one day, while vacuuming under a bed in Wellesley, Massachusetts, unable to get back up. My back froze and I was in so much pain I went to a chiropractor. I liked housecleaning, but it was taking a toll on my body. The YMCA, in Natick, Massachusetts, offered a career counseling program designed to help women over age thirty-five re-enter the workplace. Having recently turned thirty-five, I qualified for the program. My career path was littered with so many odd jobs I still had no idea what I wanted to be when I grew up. I hoped the career counseling would help me focus on work I could love. I didn't want to be a housekeeper for the rest of my life and I was running out of options. Never having been good at taking orders, it was becoming very clear I would always be self-employed.

My new counselor had me take a series of aptitude tests. After crunching the numbers, my test score was a profound shock. The numbers were heavily weighted in the art column. The test scores showed I was an artist. Not maybe was I an artist, I WAS an artist. With all the years struggling to not be the worst person in art class, I felt I should take the test over. This must be a mistake. But, there were the numbers—a few points for each of the other categories and a huge chunk of points for art. On one hand this was the best news ever. I was an artist! But, on the other hand, artists weren't known for their financial success in life unless, of course, they died. And, art jobs were not widely available.

My brilliant career counselor had me develop a few career ideas about what I wanted to do now I was officially a creative person. She then presented me with the reality (something with which I have always had a problem) of each occupation I proposed. Once faced with the reality, the career lost its appeal. While one part may have excited me, there would be another part with which I was not interested. After chucking several career fantasies in the wastebasket, we came around to talking about my experiences in college. I found myself excitedly talking about what I learned while at Pratt Institute especially my freshman year. As I spoke about classes I took and modeled for, I found I had some clear ideas about teachers. "What about teaching?" my counselor asked. Here I had just discovered I was an artist and now I should think of myself as an art teacher? This was the biggest fantasy.

With a little prodding, I heard myself talking about what I would like to teach—something like my freshman year where I learned things I didn't know I could do. I was never good with children, but the thought of teaching adults really appealed to me. What if I could be someone like Mr. Foster, Professor 3-D or King Coffin? What if I could show others like me, someone constantly struggling, how to draw? Wouldn't it be wonderful to give other "Muggles" a chance to find their magic in art? This would be the perfect revenge against Mrs. 2-D and all the other people who constantly told me how bad I was. Still, me teaching art was a bit of stretch because I was not many steps ahead of the students I would teach.

I began designing a class for nonartists—people like me with no art skills, no obvious talent, but a desire to learn. As the design began to take form, all the pieces of the past few years started to come together and make sense. I wanted to provide a class that would give my students what I never had—a good foundation in drawing. The class would be called "Beginning Art" and would encompass a taste of the art world. With exercises using pencil, crayon, pastel and watercolor, students would be introduced to the foundation of all art—drawing.

After a year of preparation using Betty Edwards's Drawing on the Right Side of the Brain, I sent out my first art class proposals and landed my first adult education job at MassBay Community College's evening program, in Wellesley, Massachusetts. I was so excited about the beginning of my new life. I finally found a focus and a place where I could be useful. My life would now be about art and everyone was going to take my classes and become artists. As we all know, the dream and the reality are not always on the same page. My class would take a turn no one could have foreseen.

Challenger

It was a Tuesday afternoon at the end of January 1986 and my first Beginning Art class was to start in one week. Every moment of everyday, since my class was first accepted, was filled with thoughts of what I would say that first night. My new life was about to begin and I was excited about the prospects. I was still cleaning houses and one of my clients required me to purchase her rum and vodka each week from her favorite, local liquor store. I was on my way to pick up her order with the radio on in my 1976 Chevrolet Monte Carlo. I had one ear to the radio because this was a big day for all of us in Massachusetts. Christa McAuliffe, a local teacher, was patiently waiting with her fellow crewmates to fly into outer space. Many people were listening to their radios or glued to their TVs.

As I pulled to the curb, the space shuttle Challenger was preparing for liftoff. The countdown began. As the rocket was launched, I began to shut off the car engine. All of a sudden the announcer was saying the Challenger had exploded. It was the last thing I heard as I turned off the car. In a panic, I quickly tried to turn it back on. This couldn't be true. Someone had made a terrible mistake. I must have heard wrong. The crew would be fine. But, I couldn't start the car. In a cloud of anxiety, I rushed into the liquor store and asked about the Challenger and if I could use their phone to call my mechanic. There were people listening to the news in the store. It was real. I felt numb with a sense of horror and disbelief as I waited for my mechanic and the tow truck.

Faced with having to come up with the money for car repairs and with my new class starting in a week, I felt a touch of selfishness in the news of the Challenger disaster. I knew from that moment on the Challenger would always be the date associated with my dream. The start of my new life would forever be entwined with the news of this unimaginable tragedy. I had finally found something that was going to be a life path and our world had just exploded. Our nation was in a profound state of mourning and signing up for art classes was the last thing anyone was interested in. My class would run with six students—the bare minimum for a class. My new class would take on a flavor I could never have anticipated.

February 4, 1986 marked the first week anniversary of the Challenger disaster. My class started at 6:30 p.m., and my new students, understandably, were very disturbed by the Challenger disaster. The small class allowed for a needed sense of intimacy. Between the exercises and my necessary jabbering, we talked. We talked about the Challenger and my students' families. We talked about why we wanted to learn how to draw and why that journey had been so difficult. My students completed the drawing exercises. I assigned reading and drawing homework, gave them a list of supplies they would need for the next class. With the first night completed, Beginning Art began.

My original syllabus was for eight weeks. We continued to share stories. My first students helped shape the class with their feedback. It seemed, with each passing week, there was a kind of healing happening in the process of creating art. I was excited and amazed, as were my students, to see drawing skills develop. I shared stories and anecdotes. I had no idea what would happen. Would the class survive? Would it do all the things I wanted it to? This sharing and healing was an outcome I had never envisioned. I stumbled a lot that first semester and for many semesters after that. But Beginning Art would now have the added bonus of "therapy." I also discovered I was learning as much, if not more, from my students, another welcome bonus. At the end of the semester, the students were now drawing like they had never dreamed possible. It was working. My dream was working. And theirs were, too.

That first memorable class way back in February 1986 set a course I could never have imagined.

After the First Class

My early teaching path was filled with constant anxiety with the approach of each new semester. Would enough students sign up to run the class? Would there be another semester or another school that would run my class? Art for everyone was a new concept and it was a time when people wanted classes that would enhance their careers, not just for enrichment.

For the next few years the story was always the same, until I found a home in the Keefe Tech Adult Ed. program, in Framingham, Massachusetts. I loved the school, the faculty and the students. The school was close to my apartment so I could get to class in five minutes. What a beautiful school. And they were happy to run my class. I always managed to teach two semesters every year, but anxiety about enrollment remained. I LOVED teaching this class and I looked forward it. My enrollment numbers were never high, but there was enough of an interest with five or six students to guarantee my course would run. Keefe Tech offered Beginning Art and, eventually, Beginning Art, part two, and a beginning portrait class, as my students showed interest. It was a great place to work on my teaching skills.

****

Part II
Helen Van Wyk

Chapter 4: How I Found Helen
Framingham Students

    After the completion of one semester of
Beginning Art, at Keefe Tech, in Framingham,
Massachusetts, my class of seven decided I should
now teach them how to paint. I explained to them I
didn't know how to paint even though I painted.
They insisted I teach them what I knew and we
would go on from there. One student found a room
for us at an American Legion Post and set
everything up. Funny how life unfolds sometimes.
Now I was a painting teacher.

    The new painting class progressed nicely.
Everyone enjoyed each other's company. We
would often start our class scribbling with crayons
on opened, brown paper bags. There were always
lively discussions and lots of laughter. My new
painting students were painting and I was learning
how to teach them. Most of the time I just made it
up as I went along, but I was surprised at what years
of taking classes had taught me. I seemed to know
enough to share stories and encourage my new
painters.

    Some of my students started to watch Helen
Van Wyk, a painter on PBS. They suggested I
watch her, too, because she said a lot of the things I
was teaching them. Being uncommonly stubborn, I
resisted. After having read many books about
painting and taking classes about painting, I was
convinced this would be just another frustrating bit
of information. My students kept insisting I watch
this painting teacher. After a year, I finally broke
down and started to watch Helen Van Wyk in her

"Welcome to My Studio" series. This was like finding a pot of gold at the end of the rainbow.

Helen Van Wyk – "Welcome to My Studio"

Helen's series was on every Saturday morning for two, half hour sessions. On that first Saturday morning, I sat in front of my television ready to be bored or feel like I wasn't a good painter. Some music played and the series opened with scenes of Helen walking her whippets. OK so far. I don't remember what episode I watched first, but I know once Helen came on the screen and began her lesson my eyes were glued on the set. I found I desperately needed to take notes. Lots of notes! And then I realized I couldn't possibly take that many notes so I decided to tape the show. In that first half hour I realized my students had given me a tremendous gift. Here were all the answers to questions I didn't even realize I needed to ask about painting. Helen had the answers to color, composition, light, and shadow. While imparting all this knowledge, Helen was entertaining and funny.

I had read books and taken classes, but no one had ever taught me the fundamentals of painting. Before I watched Helen's series, the colors didn't work or the explanations were confusing. No lightbulbs went on in my head and I was frustrated. The information from the books and classes got filed away in my mind.

I watched and taped Helen every Saturday morning. Then I watched the tape every single day until the next Saturday. I took notes. I tried her exercises. I discovered Helen had written books and, by the end of the next year, I owned all of them. Not only was Helen an amazing and gifted artist and teacher, she was also a gifted writer. My mildly dyslexic brain couldn't read fast enough. Every sentence was sustenance for my starving artist's soul. One of her books is so marked up from my highlighter there isn't much white space left on the pages.

Helen said things I needed to hear. If Helen said to use Sap Green, I went out and bought Sap Green. If she said NEVER use Cadmium Red Medium—I threw mine out. I totally adopted her palette of colors. I was learning how to put colors together and how to recognize values. I started to introduce Helen's practices to my painting class. At first, some of the transition was a bit bumpy for my students, but I felt so strongly about what I was learning it was all worth whatever struggles we had to go through.

Prior to this, I never had a palette of colors. When I took classes, we brought what we had with us and muddled through. There was no list of colors to bring. There was a lot of learning by process of elimination. Now, for the first time in my life, I was able to look at something and paint it. For years I was able to draw things, but applying and mixing color was a total mystery. I painted straight out of the tube. I called myself an abstract painter, but the truth was I didn't know how to paint anything real. Now I had a palette that could recreate everything in the known world—teapots, oranges, pine trees, skin tones, flowers, bananas, metals—ANYTHING. Helen's colors brought everything to life and applying her basic principles gave me the opportunity to make my paintings come alive. In order to digest all the information about color I was learning, I spent one four-hour trip driving to Vermont imagining what colors I would use to paint what I saw. Did that tree have Cadmium Red Light with a little Yellow Ochre mixed in? Was that evergreen a mixture of Thalo Green and Burnt Sienna? Geez! Is the road Alizarin Crimson mixed with Zinc White and Ivory Black? The exercise helped to cement my new color palette into my brain. Lightbulbs were popping everywhere in my head. Not only had I found an artist I admired, but I also found a teacher to emulate.

I had started painting in 1970. Now, twenty-two years later, I was finally learning how to paint. Up to this moment I was searching in darkness. Now, there was vision, focus, light and passion, and the special part of this was I could now share my discoveries with my students.

Helen's Classes

One day, in the spring of 1993, I decided to hunt up Helen Van Wyk. I figured she was probably like many TV personalities—totally unapproachable and probably way too expensive for me to ever see her in person. I went off to the library and browsed through the Rockport, Massachusetts's phone book. To my amazement, there was a listing for Helen and her husband, Herb Rogoff, complete with address. Not yet believing my good fortune, I assumed if I called I would end up with some voice machine telling me classes were $5,000 and already filled. I finally got up the courage to call and Herb answered. "Oh yes," he said, "we have classes here at the house every summer. They are Friday mornings at 9 until noon. Each class is $10 and you just come and watch Helen paint. You don't have to bring anything or make a reservation—you can just show up." We had a lovely chat. He was charming and answered all my questions. Then he gave me directions to their house and said he would see me Friday morning. I could not believe I was going to actually see Helen Van Wyk. I had Friday mornings off, I could afford $10 a week and Rockport was only a couple of hours away!

That Friday, I was up at the crack of dawn, determined not to sit in rush hour traffic. At 6:30 I hopped into my old, red Toyota Tercel and started off for Rockport. The trip took about ninety minutes and the traffic was not a problem. Once I arrived in Rockport, I would often buy a cup of coffee, a muffin and a newspaper at the local Dunkin' Donuts. Then, I would sit in my car in Helen's 15-car parking lot and keep myself entertained until class started at 9 a.m. I loved being in Rockport and was excited to be taking class.

****

Chapter 5: My Summer with Helen

It was June 11, 1993, a week after my forty-second birthday. This was Helen's twenty-fifth season teaching classes at her home in Rockport. I was so excited you would think I had been invited to observe Monet paint. I was always the first one in the parking lot and eventually, other cars would start to arrive. Shortly before 9 a.m., everyone would line up outside Helen's door. Herb, or sometimes Helen, would let us in. We would pay our $10 fee to their secretary at her desk just inside the door. This room contained Helen's finished works, her books, her mini-magazines and her brushes, which were all for sale.

We were led through Helen's house to an attached garage in the back. It was set up with fifty wooden chairs neatly aligned in five rows. High stools were placed along the back wall. All were facing Helen's easel and her still life to her left. She would spend the Thursday before class setting up her still life and getting her paints ready. There was a refrigerator in the garage where Helen stored her paints. She had placed a piece of paper with our names on each chair for this first demonstration. I only remember her doing this once. After that, we were on our own selecting our seats. It was quite an intimate gathering.

Helen would go to her seat at her easel, someone would turn off the main lights and Helen would begin painting. Everything was in darkness except for the 40W light on her canvas and the 100W light on her still life. At this demonstration Helen used an 18-by-24 canvas. Her 6-foot, wooden easel was tilted forward at the top to prevent glare from the light. Her canvas was higher than her eye level so we could all see what she was doing. As she painted, Helen talked and told stories. The first thing she taught us was how to pronounce her name (Wike) and said, "You don't say Dick Van Dick!" Not only was she a gifted painter, we discovered she was also a gifted entertainer, and good at making a point.

In this class, Helen's still life consisted of a tall, black vase (I promptly went out and bought one just like it), two apples and some green grapes. There were twigs with some little gray berries on them sticking out of the vase. Helen always started with a black and white acrylic underpainting. This, she explained, was what the great masters did. Pigment was very expensive. It was difficult to cover large areas with color. So, the great masters applied egg tempera in black, white and shades of gray as a first layer of paint, massing in the shapes of light and dark. Then, when it was time to apply color, the painter didn't have to use as much of the precious pigment.

Helen massed in the values of dark and light, not with a brush, but with a sponge applicator doctors use to prep patients for surgery. Helen did this for about seventy-five minutes. We were allowed to take pictures as she painted, but Helen wanted us listening and watching rather than taking copious notes. It was difficult not to write down everything she said. Every sentence out of her mouth was another pearl of wisdom. Once her underpainting was finished, Helen announced Herb had tea and cookies for us in the dining room. This gave the acrylic time to dry and time for Helen to put oil colors on her palette.

Herb had a table set up with iced tea and we could take two cookies each. We could also wander around Helen's house. The house was small, but beautiful and nicely appointed. Even with all the collections Helen had around (probably pieces from her travels) her house was never cluttered. I would have loved to have painted everything I saw. Her pieces were charming and always looked like they were purchased for some still life down the road. There was beautiful light everywhere. Helen's house sat at the top of her street. You could see the ocean only a few yards away. People were wandering everywhere in her house. When asked why she wasn't afraid someone would steal one of her treasures she said, "You can take anything you want, just leave Herb."

It was a welcoming and relaxed atmosphere. The crowd was extremely respectful of Helen's home. No one sat on the furniture. They wandered around looking at Helen's paintings. Most people came each week so it was like a large family gathering.

Imagine fifty people traipsing through her house and all having to use the bathroom! The bathroom was connected to a cesspool. We were instructed to "share a flush" so we didn't overtax the system. I never remember there being any problem.

Many of Helen's attendees had been with her since she started twenty-five years earlier and were in their seventies. Some were just starting to paint. A few of us were in our thirties and forties. We were the new kids on the block completely in awe of Helen. I drove in from Framingham. Someone else drove up from Connecticut. But, none of us could compete with the woman dressed in white who flew in from Texas every weekend!! Helen loved it.

After the break, we were herded back into the garage studio where Helen was set up and ready to apply her oil colors. I can tell you she did not tolerate stragglers. Helen was of the old school— quite strict and I appreciated that. There was no fooling around. She had work to do. We had better pay attention.

Sometimes I felt there was a need for the urgency because Helen mentioned to some of us she had cancer. She always wore a gray-haired wig and would often adjust it and scratch an itch under it while she was painting. She never did this while taping her series for TV. I always wonder when I watch her videos if the wig was driving her crazy. It was nice she was so relaxed and OK about herself. Helen had been through treatment and survived, but cancer has a nasty habit of reappearing. We all had a feeling Helen would not be with us much longer. This was our last chance to learn the mysteries of painting. Many of the people I talked with were like me—taking classes for years, but never quite "getting it" until they studied with Helen.

Helen began applying color over her black and white underpainting. Sometimes she would call out her mixtures (Helen's palette is explained in Chapter 10). Mostly, she told stories and explained what she was doing. After each step, adding dark or blending an edge, she would always ask, "Why?" And then she would explain.

While Helen didn't like us taking notes while she painted sometimes I couldn't help myself so, under the cover of darkness, in the back of the room, I jotted a few things down. I usually took three photographs, too: one of her still life set-up, one of her underpainting and one of her finished painting. The photographs are found later in this Chapter.

I don't think any of us ever correctly guessed her color mixtures. She would put the oddest combinations together and come up with the most beautiful colors. She would often tell us she had been painting for fifty years and, when we had painted for fifty years, we could paint like this, too.

At 11:45 a.m., we would start wondering if Helen would finish by noon. Her application was methodical. She worked from the top down, applying medium tones first and then adding the darker darks and lighter lights. I could never imagine finishing a painting in two and a half hours, but at the stroke of noon Helen was done. Another masterpiece. We would sit there dumbfounded. After all these years, I have yet to be able to complete a painting in that short a time. Always the showman, Helen gloried in her finished work.

Each Friday I showed up until our last session together on September 24, 1993. Helen would go to Italy or other warm places for the winter. She also had her series to film and her books to write so she held classes only in the summer. I'd like to share with you the notes I wrote down from each session. Helen's words of wisdom are in italics followed by my observations.

06/11/1993
Intensify, Simplify, Qualify

Intensify—darken the darks, lighten the lights.

Simplify—don't make it complicated and too busy.

Qualify—it needs to make sense.

Work from the inside out—stay away from the edges.

It's the center of the painting that should keep the eye interested. The edges should not be more interesting, leading the eye out of the painting.

Respect society enough to make your painting understandable.

Helen believed artists should make paintings reflect the beauty of the world. Paintings should make sense when viewed. People shouldn't have to wonder what the painting is about. I loved this comment.

Gray values—don't make them smooth.

Because she was adding a gray background, she wanted her paint strokes to reflect an atmosphere. Flat, smooth strokes would make the background less interesting.

Use a light wash of color (glazing).

Glazing was something new to me. It is the application of transparent color over paint that is dry. The glaze adds color and tone where it is applied without masking or covering the paint underneath.

Every painting presented a unique series of problems to solve. Because Helen painted so much and painted so many different things, she was vastly experienced at capturing all kinds of surfaces.

"Black vase with grapes, apples and twigs"
16-by-20 canvas

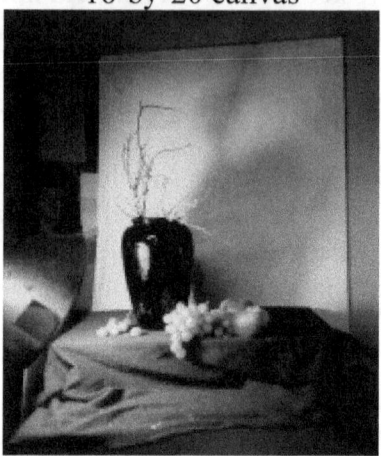

Actual still life

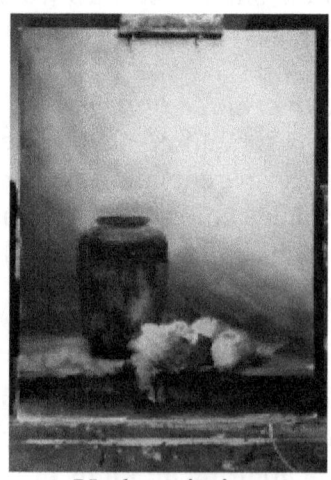

Underpainting

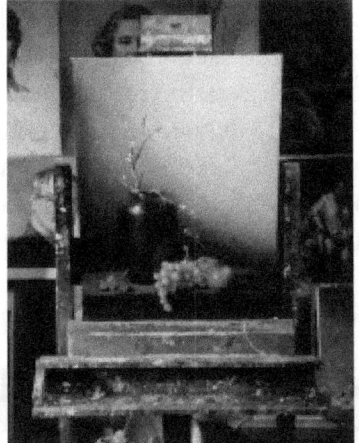
Finished painting

As we watched Helen finish this painting she said, "I think I'll paint the dust I see on the vase." Mind-blowing. I still haven't tried to paint dust yet.

***

07/02/1993
Helen's little whippet had recently died and she was distraught during this session.

If you can't adjust, don't paint!
This has to be one of my favorite Helenisms of all time! I must repeat this several times a week to my students. All parts of a painting must be open to changing and fixing right up until the painting is signed. Sometimes that means trying another color, removing or adding something.

What you put in a painting—is it effective?
The painting has to make sense. The objects in a painting have to support each other, not detract.

Helen was showing us the colors Thalo Yellow Green and Sap Green (see Chapter 10). What was interesting to watch was the lettuce wilting under the spotlight. But Helen captured the best part of the lettuce and not the eventually wilted specimen. She remembered what lettuce was supposed to look like and wasn't wedded to the objects in front of her.

"Lettuce, tomatoes, scallions and peppers"
18-by-24 canvas

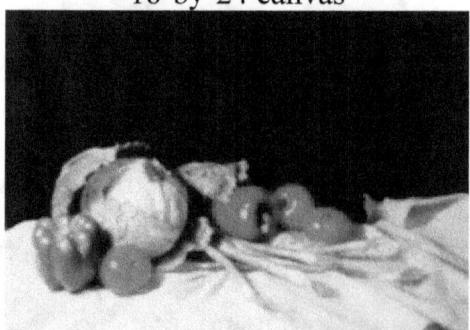

Actual still life

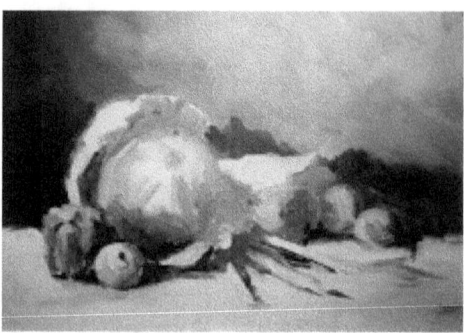

Underpainting

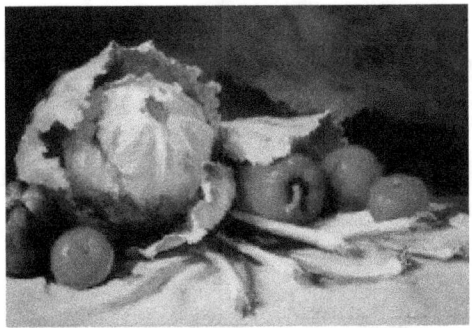

Finished painting

Helen did her paintings in class "alla prima," which means all at once. She started and ended in one sitting. I hear she often reworked paintings after we left.

***

07/09/1993

Helen did her usual underpainting in acrylic. Instead of a brush, she used a sponge applicator to apply acrylic to the background. She liked how the applicator spread the paint.

Next, she added thin layers of paint (glazes), white mixtures (scumbles) then, she worked from the top of her canvas down alla prima.

Technique is destroyed by fear.

Helen talked about this a lot. If you are gripping your brush so your knuckles are white, that tension, that panic and fear flow into your painting. Beginners often have a stiffness in their paintings reflecting their terror of making a mistake.

Helen would ask us, "What is the worse thing that could happen?" Watching Helen paint was very enlightening. She slapped the paint on. When

we considered we could paint over our mistakes or
start a new painting—we understood the point
Helen was trying to make. Relax!! It's paint.

"Wooden bucket, pears, plums and apple"
16-by-20 canvas

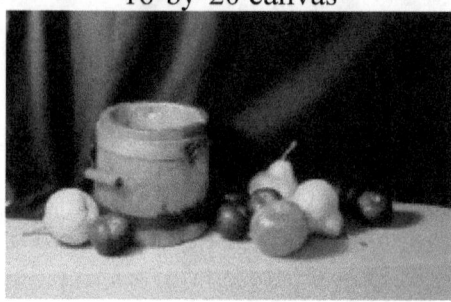

Actual still life

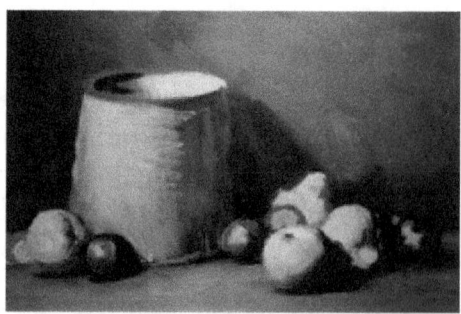

Underpainting

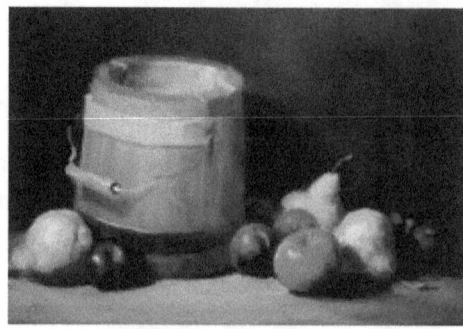

Finished painting

In this still life she used Alizarin Crimson and Thalo Red Rose to paint the plums. Not a color mixture I would have ever considered.

***

07/16/1993

Helen did a portrait of a neighborhood friend. This was the first time I got to see her paint a portrait. Many people have issues with doing flesh tones. Here is Helen's recipe:

1. Flesh is any warm color into white. Warm colors include red, yellow and orange. That includes light, medium and dark tones.

2. The basic tone of flesh is a warm color because there is blood flowing under the flesh.

3. For her flesh shadows, Helen used a mixture of Light Red, Yellow Ochre blended into black and white.

Don't worry about eyes, nose and mouth. Worry about forehead, cheeks and chin.

Students get so bogged down in the details of a painting they can't see the forest for the trees. I often see my students putting the eyes in before the head shape even exists. Our inartistic left brain often gets into the act when we paint eyes, nose and mouth by applying symbols of those objects to our painting instead of looking at what we are painting. The result is a frustrating mess that has no resemblance to the person we are trying to paint. How many times have I seen mouths with turned up edges in a painting when the actual mouth did not turn up at all?

Forehead, cheeks and chin are less interesting shapes to our left brain. Therefore, these are shapes that are the most important to paint. They are actually easier shapes to paint and provide the correct proportions to support the features. You can spend hours on features, but if the skull, cheeks, chin and neck shapes are wrong—your features will never look right. You will not get a likeness. It is not the eye color that makes someone recognizable to us. We recognize a friend walking toward us, not by the shape of his or her nose or mouth, but by the posture, the silhouette of head, shoulders and torso. It is the body shape, the stance and the head shape we need to concentrate on. If those are correct, then the features fit.

It is easier to put light into dark.

In the portrait ("Woman in a straw hat and flowered dress"), Helen put in dark and medium tones first. Then, she added light on top of them. Helen did this instinctively. She always made the tone darker than what I saw and then added the light values. I am still struggling with this technique.

"Woman in a straw hat and flowered dress"
20-by-24 canvas

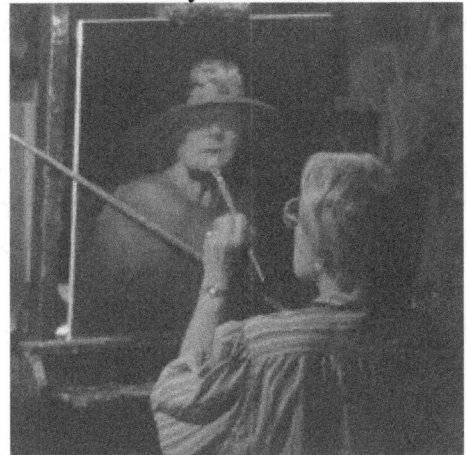

Starting the painting

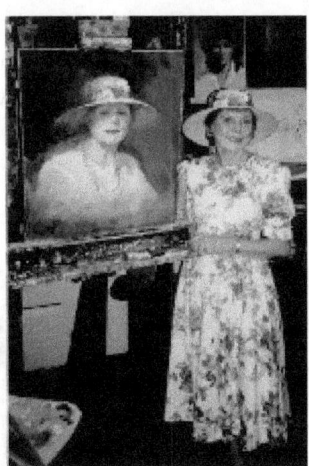

The finished product

Notice how Helen didn't put the eyes in at the beginning.

***

07/23/1993

Helen did an exquisite painting of a weed—Queen Anne's lace! I have tons of these growing in my backyard.

For the background, Helen used a mixture of Ivory Black and Indian Red. Again, two colors I would have never put together. Indian Red was not a color with which I was familiar. However, I learned it could make an awesome background! By the way, Indian Red comes from clay in India. It has nothing to do with Native Americans.

Do it wrong so you can get it right!

I loved this. Since most of us felt like we did everything wrong, Helen was once again telling us we had to do it wrong first—so we would eventually do it right!! Painting is about changes. It's like life. We don't know all the answers when we start. As the painting progresses, we correct and move and correct some more.

"Queen Anne's lace"
18-by-24 canvas

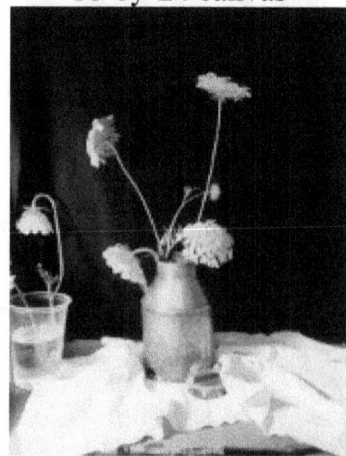

Actual still life

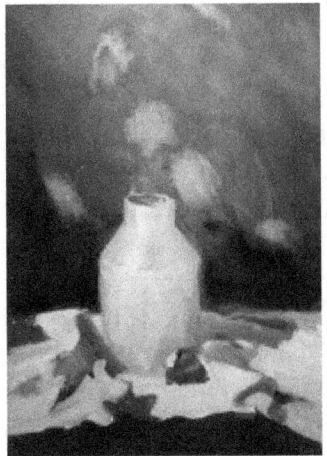

Underpainting

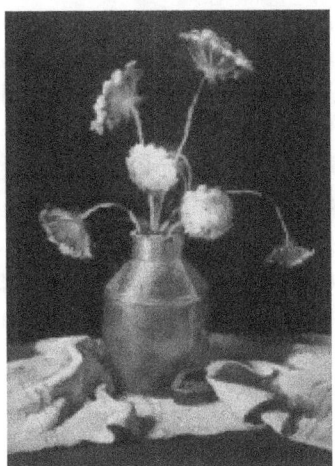

Finished painting

Helen not only taught me about painting, she taught me to see beauty in everything. She opened my eyes to a world I had never noticed.

***

07/30/1993

If I remember correctly, this was the morning Helen greeted some of us early-arrivers before class. There were maybe three or four of us standing around waiting for the others to arrive. Helen stood outside her door. I was star struck that she was standing in our presence. Here she was, in the flesh and I was only a few feet away from her.

She didn't usually greet us. It seemed obvious to me she was upset. She told us her doctors had found cancer in her body again, but they didn't know where it was. That news devastated her. That news devastated us. Even though great strides had been made in cancer research, cancer, in the 1990s, usually meant death. She had survived previous chemo for her cancer, but I didn't have a good feeling about this second round.

I still remember that day clearly. I thought it was so unfair. Helen was so full of life. She was the goddess of all things paint. How could she be taken from us? I did feel in my heart her time was not far away. I think everyone who knew her felt there wasn't much time left. Maybe that is why we sat there and tried to memorize everything she did and said.

"Watermelon"
16-by-20 canvas

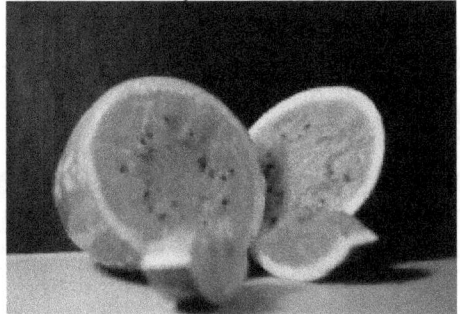

Actual still life

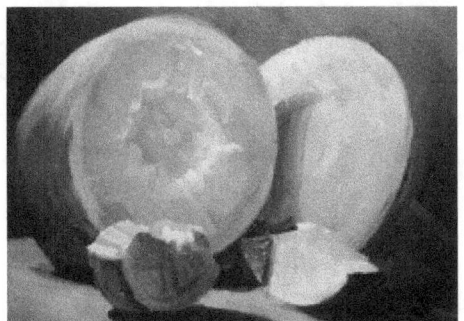

Underpainting

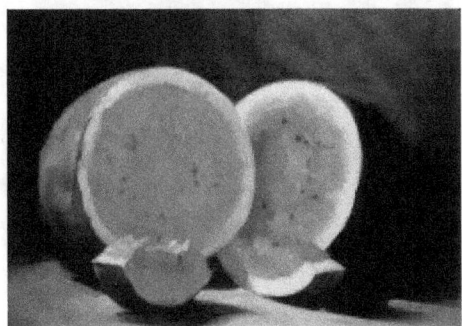

Finished painting

***

08/06/1993

Helen could pick the most complicated subject matter to paint. Things that frightened her audience were nothing to her. Helen was fearless and, I believe, that contributed to her success as a painter. In "Flowers and Corn," Helen used orange, red, yellow and violet.

Black regulates the intensity of green, blue and Alizarin Crimson—the cool colors. We don't need this for the warm colors because we have darker and duller versions of each.

Often, Helen would spray the painting with retouch varnish to work over what she had done. This would make the canvas wet and easier to paint on.

"Flowers and corn"
22-by-28 canvas

Actual still life

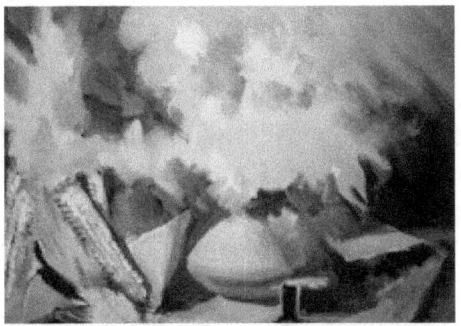

Underpainting

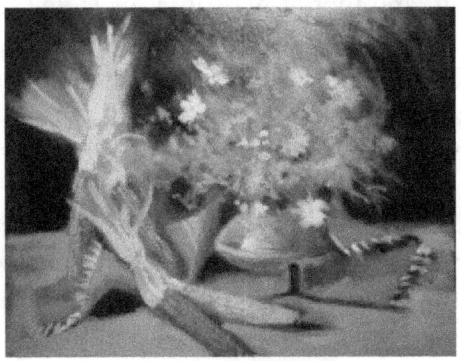

Finished painting

***

8/10/1993
Rockport Art Association

Helen often presented art demonstrations for groups in her area. I had this particular Tuesday evening off so I made a plan to drive out to Rockport and watch Helen at the Rockport Art Association. I found a little place to have dinner then drove to the venue. I actually made it there early. We didn't have GPSs in those days.

I planted myself in the front row of the 100-seat auditorium. There was a raised stage with stairs going up each side. I was nicely comfortable and excited to watch Helen paint. She would be doing a self-portrait.

Next thing I knew, Helen sat next to me. I tried to be cool, remembering to breathe. I didn't think Helen even knew who I was. There was no one else in my row, but she sat with me and we talked. I was so star struck I can't remember a word we said. I do remember I could sense she was nervous. Hell, if I had to get up in front of a bunch of strangers and do a self-portrait—I'd probably pass out! We chatted on, and then it was time for Helen to get up on stage. She was a true professional. You would never think she had been nervous as she stood in front of a crowd of 100 plus.

How I loved watching her work a crowd. She would joke and teach and explain what she was doing while she was painting. When she finished her portrait, and a splendid job it was, everyone formed a line to go up on the stage and give her his or her regards.

Never one to wait in line, I stood below Helen and off to the side of the stage so I got bits and pieces of her conversations as she spoke with each person. At one point a tall, elderly and slightly pompous gentleman began telling her what she could have done better. I stopped breathing. I couldn't believe anyone would be so rude. With a sweet, devilish smile on her face, Helen made a comment about a certain part of his male anatomy. She knew I could hear her. I choked trying not to guffaw at Helen's sweetly sarcastic comment! The gentleman looked as if he couldn't quite believe what he was hearing. Her comment shut him up and sent him on his way. And I could see how pleased she was with herself. What a woman!!!! I was so glad I was there.

You can't finish a painting until you get the start right.

 Helen spent a good deal of time getting her values, shapes and placement of shapes accurate at the beginning of her painting. She would continue tweaking, but her foundation was always strong.

When in doubt—use gray!

 Helen loved to use gray. Her gray was a mixture of black, white and a color from her palette. Helen introduced us to the beauty of gray. It was like learning about another dimension in painting.

Don't use a complement on the light side (of a portrait)! It's like digging a hole in the flesh. Use a duller yellow, red or orange. (See Helen's palette in Chapter 10).

 Since flesh is always a warm color (red, yellow or orange), its complement would be blue, green or purple—all cool colors. Using cool colors on flesh where the light is hitting makes a garish and muddy appearance. Using the darker values of the warm colors gives a more pleasing effect.

"Self-portrait"
16-by-20 canvas

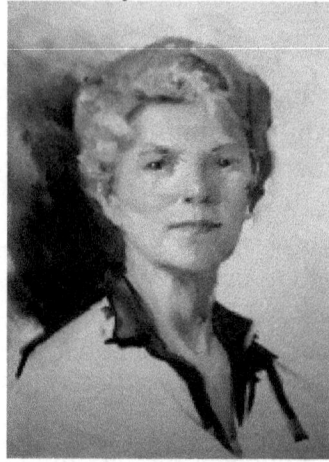

Helen's demonstration

***

08/13/1993

When I walked into Helen's studio and saw the still life she had set up I thought, this woman is either totally fearless or totally crazy. There, hanging from a board Helen had propped up, was a collection of glass balls wrapped in fishing net. The majority of people sitting in Helen's garage would never have the courage to undertake such a still life—especially if we only had two and a half hours to complete it. Helen just loved blowing our minds—which she did very successfully each and every Friday.

Helen used Mars Black for acrylic. Because it is so dense, it is great for underpainting. It covers well and makes a wonderful dark black. For this reason, Mars Black is not good for mixing color.

The world is made up of reflective and nonreflective surfaces. Anything that reflects light back to you is reflective. Glass, metal, water, apples, and glazed pottery will reflect light from their surroundings and are therefore reflective, or shiny. Fabric, cork, earth, flesh, etc. do not reflect light back. They are nonreflective.

Start the reflection with a general mass tone. In the case of the glass balls, Helen started with mass tones of the ball colors. Then, she added dark and light.

"Glass balls"
16-by-20 canvas

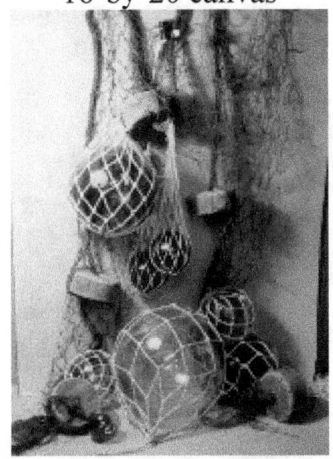

Actual still life

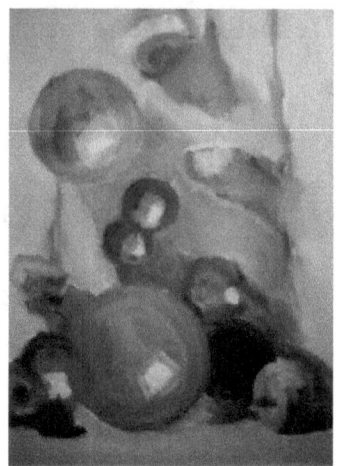

Underpainting

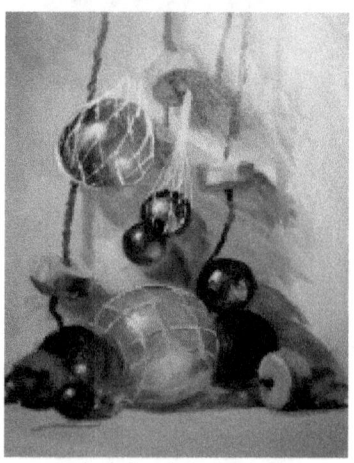

Finished painting

***

08/20/1993

    Helen took things we saw every day and turned them into an exquisite still life. The flowers in "Metal bucket and wild flowers" are common weeds. And an old metal bucket? My father had

one. I convinced him he didn't need it anymore.
That reminds me—I'd better use that bucket in a
still life soon.

Lights go on best with a big brush.
You've got to get a good amount of paint on
your brush. Big brushes can hold more paint.

"Metal bucket and wild flowers"
20-by-24 canvas

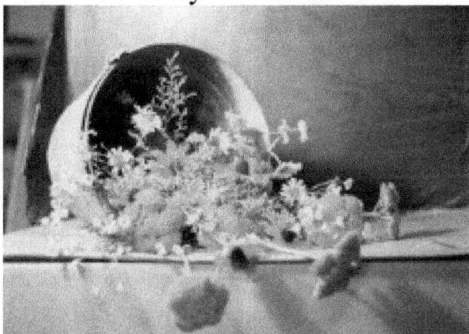

Actual still life

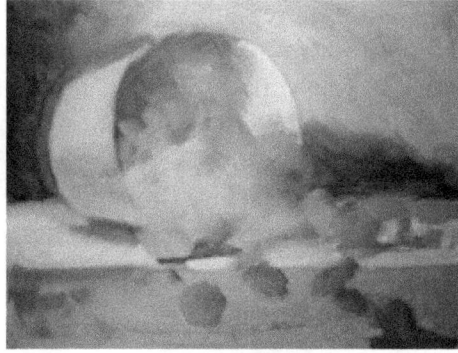

Underpainting

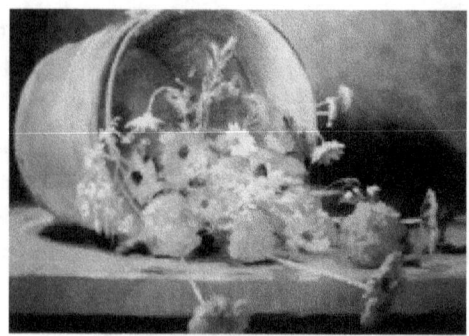

Finished painting

***

08/27/1993

The thought of sitting down to one of these complicated still life compositions would make my eyes cross but Helen simplified all the shapes and made a masterpiece. She showed us we could paint anything if we didn't go after the details first.

I happily discovered Helen continued these classes right through September. I was so excited there would be four more classes than I had expected, and at the same time I was a bit sad there were only four sessions left. Summer was quickly coming to an end.

In "Black vase and white flowers" Helen used Burnt Umber and Burnt Sienna in the background.

"Black vase and white flowers"
16-by-20 canvas

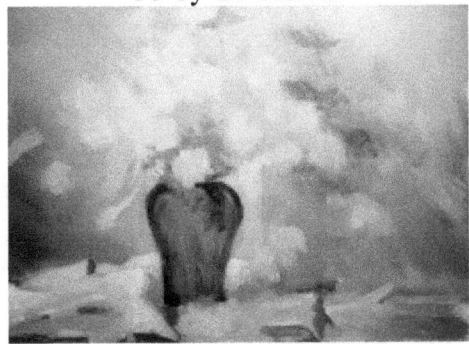

Underpainting

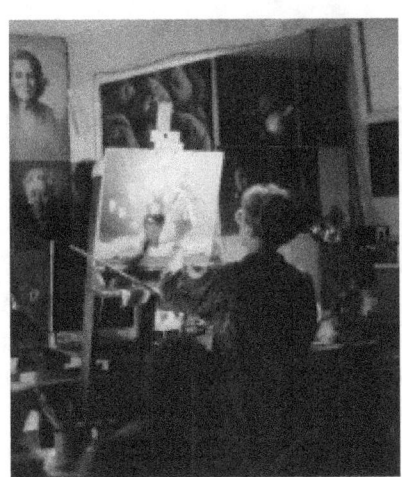

Helen at her easel

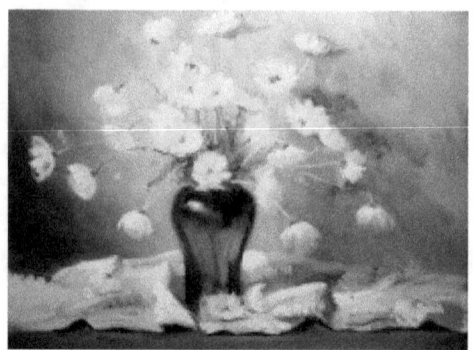

Finished painting

***

09/03/1993
Keep your studio in neutral shades.
    A neutral background won't compete with the colors of your paintings.

Any shiny surface: Stroke in one direction, then stroke in the opposite direction.
    This is a most fascinating concept. Applying strokes in both directions actually makes an object look more three-dimensional. It's like magic.

Shadows cast by objects are darker where they start.
    Which would be where they attach themselves to the object casting the shadow.

Pat on highlights—don't stroke!
    Sometimes stroking color on takes off paint. Helen used a good brush full of paint to dab on her highlights.

"Palette and paintbrushes"
20-by-24 canvas

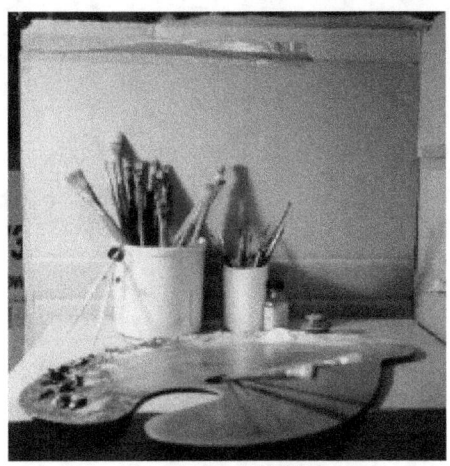

Actual still life

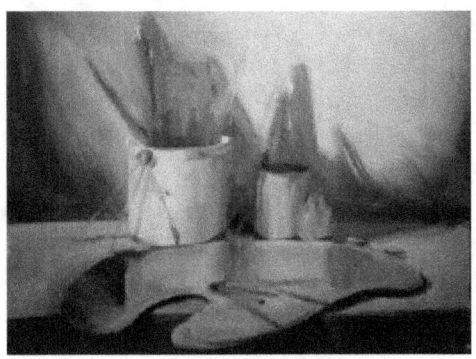

Underpainting

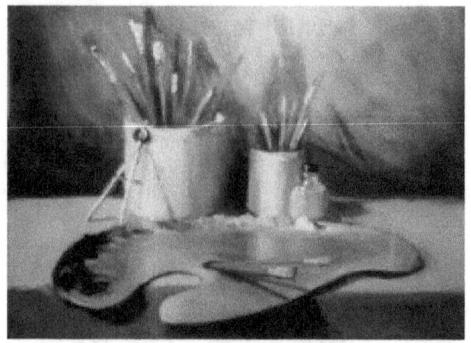

Finished painting

***

09/10/1993

On this Friday, Helen set up an exquisite basket of roses. I believe she got these from one of her neighbors. I was not good at painting flowers. Helen felt she was not good at painting roses. Her theory was, if you weren't good at painting something, it simply meant you needed to paint it more. So Helen painted roses. With her brushstrokes, Helen created the woven texture of the basket.

As we watched Helen, we were thinking how difficult this would be. Helen never thought that way. She applied her principles to everything she painted. She felt if she could paint this—we could paint this.

Work from the top down or furthest back to forward.

I'm still working on this. I can never concentrate on one area for very long.

Flowers—paint the back of them first.

It is always best to paint the background before adding the foreground. If I paint a beautiful still life before I add my background, I will have to go back and paint around and in-between my still life and shadows. This has the effect of making the objects look like they are part of a coloring book with ridges of paint around the edges of the objects. By painting the back of the flower (the part of the flower farthest from you) first, it is easier to lay the front petals (the part of the flower closest to you) on top of the back petals—and more natural looking.

Paint flowers loosely—
  Use just a suggestion of petals.
  Paint big vague shapes.
  Use lines to indicate petals.
  Go from sharp to blurry.
  Never overmix bright colors—it deadens them.

"Roses in a basket"
16-by-20 canvas

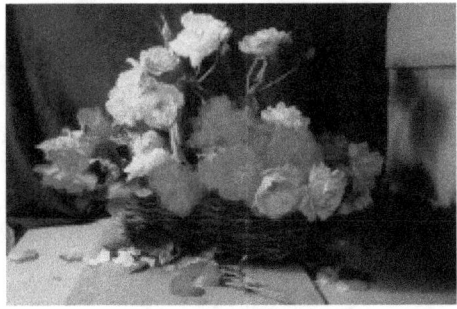

Actual still life

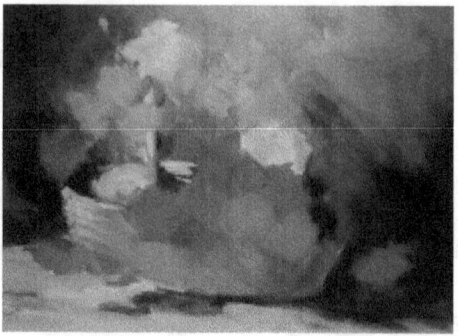

Beginning of the painting

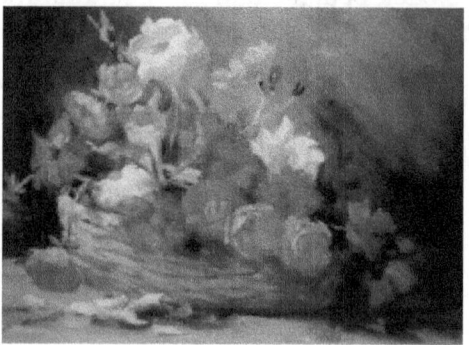

Finished painting

***

09/17/1993

Ah, white! I am in awe of white. Of course, it's not just white. That would be too easy. White always has to have another color mixed into it.

One of Helen's favorite stories was about a woman she once had in her class. The woman wanted to know how to make a mixture to portray the color white in the still life she was observing. Helen asked what color the woman saw. She answered, "off-white." Helen asked the woman the same question a couple more times and the woman continued to tell her the color was off-white. In great frustration Helen retorted, "Then put some off in it!"

To her underpainting Helen added a glaze (thin coat of paint) of Raw Sienna and Burn Umber. She did the little sugar bowl first. I never saw that one coming because I thought she would paint her back pot first. Then she painted the white pot. For her shadows she grayed white blue into violet.

When she was done, Helen stroked a darker glaze across the top of the drapery to darken it—to keep the viewer's eye from wandering off the top of the canvas—then she blended the values together so there would not be a sharp line of demarcation. After all these years, I'm still trying to do a decent white painting. I just need to keep practicing.

"White drapery and white pot"
18-by-24 canvas

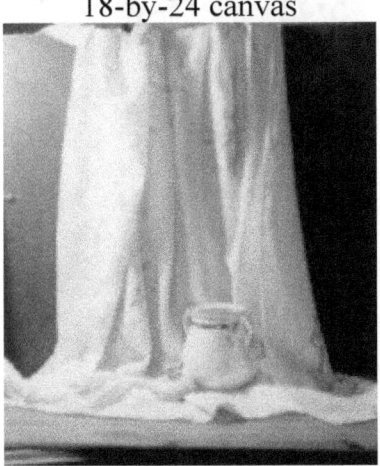

Actual still life

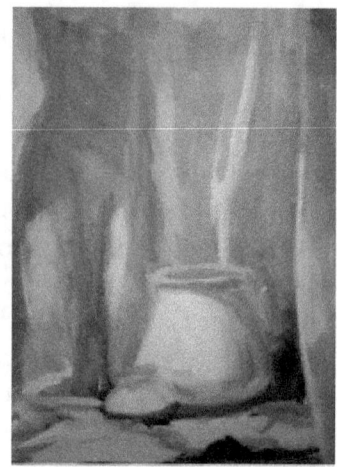

Underpainting

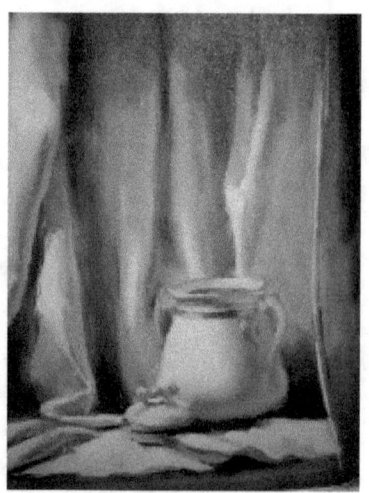

Finished painting

***

09/24/1993

Using a basket of stuffed toys as an example, Helen went over everything with us again:
1. Place objects.
2. Define objects.

3. Add tones.

4. Glaze in the medium tones.

5. Paint over the glaze in lights.

6. Develop the picture by adding more light.

7. Put color back in the shadow because of reflection—so your shadows won't look too flat.

8. Save lightest lights for last.

9. Remember to work from the top down.

10. Red is the complement/opposite color of green; blue is the complement/opposite color of orange; yellow is the complement/opposite color of violet.

She made the background rougher to be in keeping with the texture, or fur of the toys.

"Basket of stuffed toys"
20-by-24 canvas

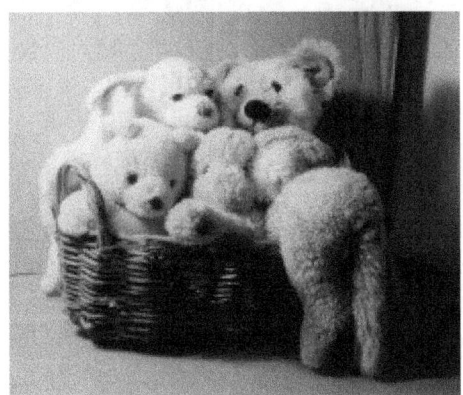

Actual still life

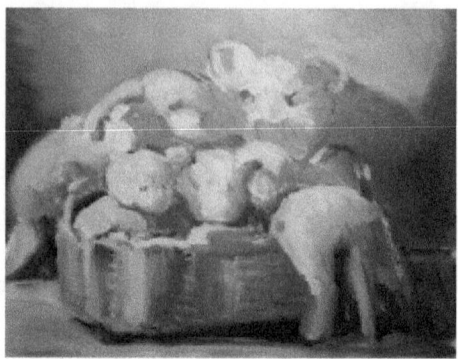

Underpainting

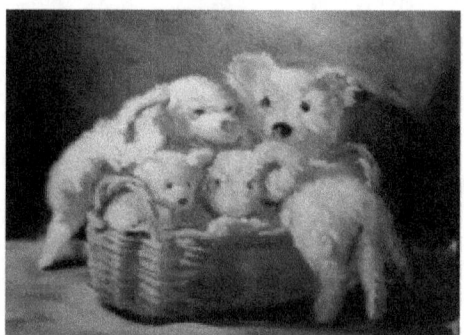

Finished painting

***

After each of Helen's summer classes, we were blown away by her talent and showmanship. Still, I would go home and paint because, as Helen said when she turned to us during one of our last sessions, "I'm the only one getting better here! If you want to get better, you have to paint!" And paint I did.

This was our last session. It was so hard to let go of the most wonderful summer I had ever had. It was the summer that changed my life.

Helen passed away in December 1994 from cancer. It is now the second decade of the twenty-first century. I still grieve for her. Helen did not know me by name. She probably wouldn't have recognized me if I met her on the street. I have lost many friends and relatives along my path, but Helen is the only one for whom I still cry. It is a deep and wrenching sense of loss from which I have never recovered. I miss her so much. She gave me more than she could have ever imagined. She sits on my shoulder when I teach my classes. She guides me when I paint. I often ask myself, what would Helen do? And I find my answers.

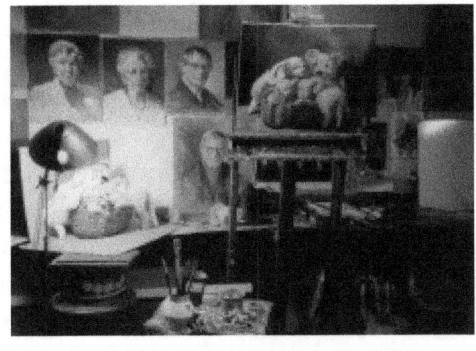

****

Chapter 6: From Framingham to Worcester
Home at Last

I will never forget that summer with Helen in Rockport; it changed my life in more ways than one.

It was while I was in Rockport I decided it might be time for me to buy a house!! Considering my artist's lifestyle, self-employed status and lack of money, this was a rather farfetched idea. I had been an apartment resident for twenty years. Owning a home was a romantic fantasy.

My living situation was becoming dangerous in Framingham. The police were visiting my apartment building and the adjacent building three to four times a week. On the days the police didn't come, the fire department did. My building was home to prostitutes, drug addicts and a wide array of drunks—most of them destructive.

It took a couple months of looking at fantasy houses before I could finally understand the actual cost of a home. I had no money to make repairs so my house had to be move-in ready. At my financial level, the options were discouraging, but the environment where I was living pushed me out to find a new home.

I found a house on a postage stamp-sized piece of property, in Milford, Massachusetts, for $72,000. I was in love. My loan was approved. I took measurements, photographs, and imagined my every waking moment in my new house. I would finally escape the war zone in which I was living. Then, three days before my closing, the bank's attorney called and informed me my lovely house had no title. That meant the bank would not OK the purchase and I would not move into the house.

This was a devastating blow. My heart was broken. I thought I would never own a home and felt utterly defeated.

One night around midnight, some idiot started a fire in the building next to me. My neighbors and I had to evacuate. It was February. It was about zero degrees outside. I put my two cats in their carrier, and picked up my two downstairs neighbors and we rode around in my warm car until 2 a.m., when the police allowed us back into our building. Things were not getting better. I had no choice but to pick up the pieces and start looking for a house again.

My real estate agent, Jill, called me about houses in Worcester, Massachusetts. "Worcester!! Why would I want to live in Worcester?" She patiently explained there was nothing left in my price range. We had to start looking west of Route 495. So off we went, two weeks after losing my lovely house in Milford, to Worcester.

It was one of those sinus migraine days in New England—sort of raining, sort of cold, snow everywhere, gray and miserable. Jill found two houses for me. House number one was on a steep hill. I'd never be able to get my car up that hill during one of our brutal New England winters. Half the house was under construction and I couldn't afford to put it back together.

We arrived at house number two. My migraine was preventing me from seeing out of one eye. As we approached the driveway entrance, we saw it had not been cleared. There was a big pile of partially frozen snow blocking the driveway I was sure we could not surmount with a vehicle. Undaunted, Jill backed her van up a few yards to get a good, running start (fortunately there were no other cars on the road). She hit the gas, up the bank we went and down a long driveway covered in ice with a large tree growing in the middle. I screamed all the way down. When we were breathing again, having missed hitting the tree, we got out of the van.

In front of us was a sad looking house painted an ugly shade of gray with black trim. We walked onto the deck. It had a gaping, rotted hole in it. Jill unlocked the front door and we walked into a cold that went right to my bones. The owners had declared bankruptcy so I was looking at a bank-owned house. This, Jill told me, would be the best deal for what I could afford.

I checked the bathroom to make sure it had a tub. I now had lots of house hunting experience and yes, I had seen a house with no tub or shower. This house had a tub, hardwood floors and a detached, one-car garage.

We decided to check out the cellar. When I opened the door, I was greeted by a stairway with steps about 4 inches wide. A child would have had trouble walking down them. At the bottom of the stairs was a broken sump pump. I envisioned falling down the stairs, hitting my head on the cement wall and then impaling myself on the pump. But, I didn't have to worry about going all the way down into the cellar because it was filled with water. The kicker was when I saw the water move.

I was slowly losing sight in my other eye due to the damn sinus migraine. I was so cold I couldn't stop shaking. I ran back up the stairs and told Jill "we are out of here!!!" It was so depressing. On our way home, she explained there were no places left in my price range. I would have to make a choice or wait.

My sister suggested I go back to look at the house wearing several layers of clothes. Jill picked me up and off we went to see the house again. There was no ice in the driveway this time. It had a huge backyard facing a tiny bit of woods. There was new sump pump installed and the cellar was almost dry. A contractor was installing a new gas furnace.

I walked around upstairs and started to imagine the changes I could make—mostly adding a fresh coat of paint to lighten up the interior. It had beautiful light and there were windows everywhere. At this point I realized this was my house! There was a half-acre of land in a lovely neighborhood on the edge of Worcester. I was preapproved for a mortgage, so we just had to pass papers. To make a long story short, I paid $71,000 for my little house and moved in April 21, 1994.

Classes in the Cellar

Worcester was a good thirty-five minutes to an hour from my various teaching and cleaning jobs. I knew it was a matter of time before I would have to move my work closer to my new home. I adored my students. It was traumatic to think of leaving them.

Amidst removing wallpaper, painting rooms and digging up an endless array of rocks in my yard, I began teaching locally at Night Life, an adult education program in Worcester, and eventually some of these students continued their studies with me at my home. My garage and cellar became my new art classrooms. The cellar had a separate entrance from the driveway and was a good size for the winter months (as long as it stayed dry), but it offered very little heat and we almost froze trying to paint there.

I finally broke down and had a gas stove installed to heat our winter classroom. Once I got over the shock of the cost, I started to enjoy the new, comfortable room. I also discovered the cellar was cool during the hot summer months. So the cellar became my studio and classroom year 'round.

Assabet After Dark

A few years after moving into my house, it was a stroke of luck I was accepted to teach at the Assabet After Dark program, in Marlborough, Massachusetts. Assabet Valley Regional Technical High School is only twenty minutes from my house. I love the school and love working with the evening division administrators. When I first started, they gave me chances to run my class even when I didn't have many students sign up. The beginning art class eventually became consistently filled with new adult artist wannabees. Assabet draws students from a large area of Central Massachusetts. My class was expressly designed for people who felt they had no talent, but had always wanted to learn to draw and paint. As I always say, "No talent required!"

In the Assabet class we cover the basics of drawing, learning to "see" like an artist. We work with collage/mixed media to begin understanding how to arrange shapes. There is a little introduction to pastels and watercolors. We cover perspective, negative space, portraits and working with light.

Interspersed with the major components of my program are stories about where I am coming from and bits and bobs I learned in my long years of trying to be an artist. They get all the basics that were missing from my education.

During the ten-week course, my students learn to develop a composition, add shadows, and work in charcoal. They learn about color. They learn about what to do if they decide to take class at any of the area art schools. They transform from terrified students on the first night to knowledgeable artists by the last class. From there students can continue their studies with me at my house, in my artsy, warm cellar.

As I settled more in Worcester and Assabet classes started to fill up, more students opted to continue studying with me at my house. Slowly, I was replacing my house cleaning jobs and art classes I taught in Concord, Framingham and Lexington with my own classes in Worcester. I had been teaching an adult painting class in Lexington, a children's art class in Concord and a beginning art and painting class in Framingham. As gas prices rose, I was able to cut a considerable amount of driving time out of my schedule.

At first, there were only one or two classes at my house. Now, I teach seven. In time, the classroom got painted and insulated. The original gas stove fell apart and was replaced with one that had an adjustable thermostat. When I replaced my kitchen cabinets the old ones became storage for my students' supplies. I had some old metal bookshelves. They got turned on their sides and attached to the cellar joists making great storage for students' paintings.

Because I have a bit of property in front of my house, I spent one summer digging out the driveway to make it circular for easier access. Everyone has a place to park off the street. The classroom space can hold seven students. There is a relaxed air of intimacy and I get to paint while they paint. We get to know each other. We chat. We share stories. We share insights, books we've read, movies we've seen and everything in between. I find it very much like having an extended family.

Over the years, students, my father and my neighbors have given me plants for my garden. When I first moved in, the half-acre of yard was mostly lawn. Since then, I have cut paths here and there, planted trees and flowers, fought poison ivy and moved rocks. I have a lot of rocks. I had a lot of poison ivy. Now, I have a lot less lawn, but an abundance of beautiful flowers.

Each spring, I collect flowers from my garden and paint a still life or two. My students meander down the path to the classroom watching the changes in the garden as the seasons progress. It has truly become a little bit of heaven and inspiration.

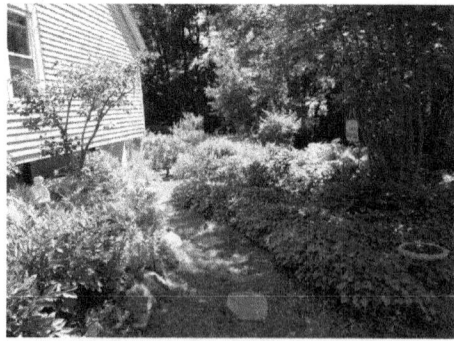

The path to the art studio

Sometimes I feel my students teach me more than I teach them. I am so blessed they share their lives with me. Recently, they had a major art show in Hudson, Massachusetts, and were so well-received, they have been invited back to show their work. As one of them said to me, "I never thought I would be good enough to show a painting." Words cannot describe how proud I am of my students.

It is because of my students I now show my work. They gently push me to explore new venues. It is because of them I designed and built my current website: http://www.kathleenhebertartist.com Now this is a path I never dreamed or desired to go down! Thank goodness for a series of "Dummies" books! But here I am, designing web pages, writing blogs, posting on Facebook and writing a book. Oh, yes, and being an artist and an art teacher!

It has been a long, challenging path, but worth everything I had to go through to get here. This part of my life is just beginning and I am looking forward to more classes, more wonderful students, more shows and maybe even more sales!

If you want to learn to draw—you can. If you want to learn to paint—you can. Buy a house? Build a website? Sell a painting? You can.

When I started drawing and painting, I could never imagine I would one day paint a landscape. This is where my path has led me....

The Red Chair

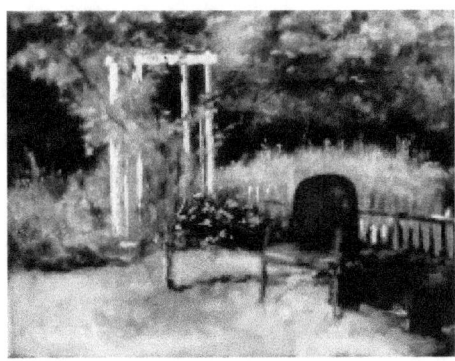

92

The next section of the book is about things I think you might need or want to know as a developing artist. There are a lot of basic bits that often make a tremendous difference in how we draw and paint. I hope you will find these helpful on your journey.

Part III
Tools, Tips and Techniques

Chapter 7: Talent is Not Required
Myths about Art

There are a lot of myths about creating art. In the past it was thought only the gifted were blessed with the ability to express themselves on paper or canvas. With the advent of Betty Edwards's book *Drawing on the Right Side of the Brain*, anyone could learn to experience what was once available only to someone with "talent." Going a step further, my teacher, Helen Van Wyk, made it possible for mere mortals to learn the basics of painting. In my opinion, desire and commitment to learn the basics combined with practice are more important than talent.

Learning to Play the Piano

Talent is not required to learn how to draw and paint and yet most people do not believe this. Can anyone learn to play the piano? Of course, you say. As long as a person is willing to put in the hours of practice needed, anyone can learn to play the piano. Do you need to be talented before you take piano lessons? Of course not, you say. You have to learn to play the piano before you discover if you have a talent for it. And, if you develop a skill for playing the piano, you might enjoy playing and learning it whether or not you have talent. So why is the scenario so different for learning to draw and paint? "I can't possibly take an art class because I have no talent," is an often heard statement. If you have never been taught basic art principles, if you haven't been instructed in the proper way to hold a pencil when you draw, which is different from how you hold a pencil when you write, how can you know if you are talented or not? And why is talent a prerequisite? Do you need talent to learn how to sail a boat before you "learn the ropes?" Do you need talent to sew before you understand how to use a sewing machine?

Talent is not required to learn to play an instrument, or to dance or draw. All that is required to learn a new skill is commitment, enthusiasm, energy, discipline, instruction and supplies.

What is Talent?

What is talent? When it comes to art, many people think talent is the ability to wake up in the morning and whip out a magic paintbrush, which allows beauty and magic to flow through us in an endless stream onto our canvas with no effort whatsoever. It's not like that. There are years of struggle, heartbreak and disappointment behind the great artists who were and are supposedly talented. And sometimes, it doesn't matter if you are talented. It can come down to politics—who you know, or luck—being at the right place at the right time. Besides, great artists aren't usually discovered until after they die. That's why I love painting so much. The pressure is off. I don't have to worry about "making it" in this lifetime. Talent is not important.

If we struggle with drawing and painting, we assume we have no talent. I have had students who do themselves a terrible disservice by showing up once a week for art class and then expecting to be able to create a masterpiece like the Sistine Chapel. They struggle with a subject they have never painted before or a technique they have never used and then beat themselves up for not being talented enough to move through the required exercise with grace and ease.

Talent isn't something magical. It is something an artist works on over the course of many years. Playing a piece of music requires time and effort to make it presentable. A painting or drawing requires the same discipline practiced over time before it can manifest as more than a childlike doodle.

Dance requires learning basic steps and rhythms so we don't look like an out-of-control maniac on the dance floor. I remember taking ballet class in college. A talented ballerina would take the class with us. She was obviously being groomed for greater things, but she was there with the amateurs doing the same exercises and stretches. Then, she would dance with the next class and the next class after that. She took as many classes each day as possible. Was she talented? Does it matter? The point is she worked at her craft. Whether she had a gift or not, she worked, and worked hard, to learn and develop skills. Talent is not required, but a commitment of time and energy is.

I have been painting for more than forty years. I wasn't talented when I started and I'm not talented now. I simply work at my craft. I have experienced suffering, failure, disappointment and ridicule, but I love to paint. I don't need talent. I don't need another reason to paint. It is my therapy, my healing, and my rest from the craziness of the everyday world. My message to all of you is if I can do it—so can you. Talent is not required.

****

Chapter 8: Draw Now Paint Later
What's First?

Where do we start? We start with the basics of learning to draw. Drawing tools are relatively inexpensive and only moderately messy. You can learn everything you need to know about seeing something and then putting it on paper by learning to draw. It is the best way to learn to translate a 3-D subject to a 2-D surface (paper). It is the foundation of the painting mediums: pastel, watercolor, oil and acrylic.

You must learn to draw before you learn to paint. Without basic drawing skills, painting will be a nightmare. Painting is drawing with a brush. You cannot jump right into painting with no basic skill. If you cannot execute a blind contour drawing, if you don't know what negative space is, or are unfamiliar with composition and values, then you will drown when you start to paint. If you can't draw the perspective of a chair in pencil, picking up a paintbrush is not going to magically impart this skill to you. You must first learn how to "see" like artists see. The best place to do this is with a good drawing class where you will learn all the fundamentals, which will assist you in drawing everything.

We, who draw and paint representational art, must translate the world of 3-D onto a 2-D canvas or sheet of paper. There is no going in or out on a canvas or sheet of paper. We are simply limited to moving up, down and sideways. Seeing how objects recede into the background requires us to restructure our thinking so we can properly translate the idea of space. Instead of asking ourselves if the object goes back, we ask ourselves if the object is higher or lower than the object we are relating it to.

Color is a whole 'nother can of worms. You don't want to be learning drawing and painting at the same time. Learn perspective, values, develop your eye, understand the magic of negative space and then you will be ready to add color to the mix.

After my students have learned basic drawing skills in my beginning art class and are making their first attempts at painting, I always ask them if they now think they should have started with painting instead of drawing. The answer is always a resounding "NO!" You have to be able to draw a barn in order to be able to paint a barn. If you can't draw a book, you can't paint a book either. Learn to draw first.

Read a Book

One of the best ways to learn how to draw is to find a copy of Betty Edwards's *Drawing on the Right Side of the Brain*. This is an excellent book for anyone wanting to learn how to draw or for anyone who has missed a few steps in his/her drawing instruction. My students are all required to do exercises from this book before they start my painting class. It is a good place to develop your "seeing" and understanding of the way the artist brain perceives things. This book is about learning the language of seeing. Looking at a 3-D object requires a visual translation in order for it to be transferred onto a 2-D flat surface. Art, like music, has a language, too. This book will help you to see like an artist. It is the foundation from which everything is possible. Once you master the techniques and become familiar with the art terms in this book, you can then move on to other artistic expressions with confidence. You need a good foundation in drawing before painting. This book is the best place to start.

I have a left and a right brain? Yes, and both work independently of each other. The left brain is our dominant half. It allows us to talk and count and is the side we educate. It is linear. The right brain is about feeling, sensing, and spatial relationships. The left brain counts off the seconds in a day. The right brain loses all sense of time. The left brain is all about symbols. It is not interested in looking at something long enough to draw it. When asked to draw a hand, it produces a circle with five lines sticking out. A left-brained face would be similar to a smiley face. The left brain cannot draw. And, because it is visually and verbally dominant, it is good at talking us out of sitting down and drawing and painting for a few hours. The left brain must shut down in order for us to correctly perceive and draw a chair, or a face, or a landscape. It does not like to be shut down and deprived of its power. Betty Edwards's book explains the techniques for overriding the left brain. My three favorites are: drawing or painting upside down, negative space and using a mirror. I will explain the use of these tools later in the Chapter.

Note: It is wise to use Betty Edwards's book in conjunction with a class. Sometimes the techniques can be confusing to the new artist, and it is beneficial to have an experienced teacher help with this stage of your journey. Many of my students said they tried to do the book exercises on their own, but were lost without instruction. Find a teacher.

Take a Class

Lots of classes are available that use *Drawing on the Right Side of the Brain* as a textbook. I find we are more inspired to draw and paint if we have to make a commitment to show up for a class. Life is always interfering and most of us won't sit down to draw or paint if we have yard work, laundry, our children or a baseball game distracting us. It's also a good idea to see other people struggling, too, so you can see you are not alone. Sharing with classmates really helps the learning process.

A local adult education program is a great place to start or ask your local arts and crafts store to recommend a class. Find a teacher who specializes in beginners. Not all teachers can handle students starting from scratch even though they may advertise a beginning class. Get a recommendation from someone who has taken the class.

Here is an example of the course description for my "Beginning Art" class at Assabet Valley Regional Technical School, in Marlborough, Massachusetts: "Nonartists only!! Talent is not required! If your lifelong dream has been to learn how to draw and paint, but you are always held back by a feeling that you have no talent—this is the class for you. First and foremost, we will take the fear out of basic drawing, the building block of art. We will explore shapes, perspective, and portraiture. We will develop our creativity, composition, and color sense in a nonthreatening, fun atmosphere. We will dispel art myths and learn to 'see' as artists see. This class is a good foundation for any of the painting mediums (watercolor, oil, acrylic, and pastel)."

Who knows? Maybe I will see you in class one day. To begin drawing, a few tools are needed.

Drawing Tools

Erasers

Pink pearl or Staedlter erasers are good for large areas. A kneaded eraser can be squished into a ball and then pinched into various thicknesses to erase tiny areas. It's also good to clean your hands and serves as a good antianxiety tool. You have to knead it to warm it up and soften it.

Tip: Draw by holding the pencil halfway down its shaft (instead of right at the tip). This makes you draw softly, hence, less need to erase.

Paper

The weight of the paper makes a difference to the drawing experience. The lower the weight (paper is labeled in pounds), the lesser the quality of the paper. Seventy-five-pound paper is not as nice as 100-pound paper. Once you start gaining confidence, you might want to try a nicer paper and see how it feels. The nicer papers are easier to erase. All purpose paper is good for beginners.

Pencils

Use soft pencils that don't look like they belong in an office. You've got to get into the artistic mood when you draw. So use graphite pencils (they don't have erasers on the end). Begin with a number 3 or 4 B pencil. "B" means soft. The higher the number, the softer and darker the pencil lead. "H" means hard. This is like drawing with a stick. The line an H makes is very light and you have to press down hard to get a decent, dark line. Learn to use a soft pencil. You can make light lines with it by applying light pressure and dark lines or shapes by applying a harder pressure. It's a good deal; one pencil for two jobs.

Drawing Techniques

Mirror

Learning to see is the artist's lifelong challenge. When we stay focused for long periods of time on our canvas or drawing without turning away, we often become blinded to that which we need to see. Use a mirror to look at your work to give you a reversed view of your artwork. This is another way to disconnect from the emotional attachment we all have to our pictures. I stand with my back to the canvas and look into a good-sized hand mirror (much like a trick sharpshooter). I gaze into the mirror and search for areas, lines or colors that are not as they should be. Sometimes it reflects my crooked perspective. Sometimes it shows me I have one eye up too high on a portrait. Sometimes it shows me a glaring color in only one area of my canvas. All these things are sometimes hard to notice when looking directly at your drawing or painting. Using a mirror this way is much like having an art teacher handy.

Negative space

Negative space is an area for which the left brain has no symbol. If you want to draw or paint something—don't name it. Don't draw an eye. Draw the white around the iris. Draw the shape between the brow and the eyelid. Draw the shapes on the cheek and the temple, but don't draw the eye! The left brain wants to draw an eye like one found in Egyptian hieroglyphics. It will demand you draw its symbol and will fight with your right brain to take control. It responds to words. Change your words to something less descriptive. "This makes an angle, this is a pointy shape, this has a round edge, and this is a fat shape with a bump on it." Keep your self-talk ambiguous.

Negative space is as important as the object you are drawing. If you draw the inside of a teacup, the outside will be correct. If you draw the space inside the handle, the outside will be correct. If your negative space is wrong—your subject will also be wrong. Learn to make negative space your friend. This is one of the greatest tools you will ever have in your attempt to draw and paint.

Upside Down

If you are working from a photo, it is extremely helpful to turn both the photo and the drawing upside down. Seriously. By turning your 2-D subject matter upside down, your right brain is engaged in drawing the shapes and relationships. The dominant, unhelpful left brain shuts off.

You should hear all the left-brained complaining and resistance when I suggest this to my students. By turning your work and your photo upside down, you disconnect from the emotional attachment you have to your work. You can now look at things through an objective eye. You can let go of your expectations and simply draw what you see, instead of drawing what you think you see.

Values

The last thing you should learn before you jump into color are values. Values mean how light or dark a color is. The reason we can see objects is because they are placed against backgrounds that contrast with their value. A light object against a dark background shows up really well. A light object on a light background disappears.

I love painting anything red. But first I have to decide is the red lighter where it's hit by light? Does it transition into medium red and then into dark red when it goes into shadow? One red isn't going to do the trick. Without the value changes, the object I'm painting would simply look flat. It's really not about the color. It's more about how light or dark the color is.

Helen taught me about values. This was a magical key to the painting process. I once wanted to make something lighter so I kept adding white to the object. In my frustration, it wasn't getting lighter. Finally, my inner art teacher instructed me to make the surrounding area darker so the white would show up more. There was no way the white could get whiter. Once I darkened the surrounding area—the light popped. I'm slow, but I get there. Thank-you, Helen.

My drawing students work with values in charcoal in the last two sessions of my beginning drawing class. I set up each of the five basic shapes: sphere, square, cylinder, cone and rectangle. Then they apply the five principles of light:

1. Body tone—the value or color of the object.

2. Body shadow—the shadow on the object.

3. Cast shadow—the shadow cast onto the surface the object is resting on.

4. Reflected light—the light bouncing on the object from the surface.

5. Highlight—pinpoints of light on the concavities and convexities in line with the light.

After my students complete their course in drawing, I have them do a painting in black and white acrylic. I set up a still life for them. They must paint it using only shades (values) of black, white and the many shades of gray. Once they are halfway through their painting, I have them switch to black and white oil to give them the experience of painting with both mediums. Oil paint can be applied on top of acrylic, but not vice versa.

Now they have tried both acrylic and oil paint, they are ready to purchase their colors. It is a bit of an investment so they can continue painting with black and white acrylic or oil until they feel ready to choose. Once they decide which type of paint they want to use, I give them a list of colors (see Chapter 10).

Viewfinder
A viewfinder for drawing and painting is much like a viewfinder on a camera. It can be a piece of cardboard with a rectangle cut in it (or a square if your canvas is square). It helps you isolate what you want to draw or paint. If you are working outside on a landscape or inside on a still life, the viewfinder helps to position your composition so you can replicate your subject in larger form onto paper or canvas. It is helpful if you have midpoints on your viewfinder—top, bottom and sides. Mark your paper or canvas with midpoints as well. I find using a viewfinder and midpoints extremely valuable. It is a great way to check the placement of my composition. When I am working from one of my photographs, I put midpoints on them. In *Drawing on the Right Side of the Brain*, Betty Edwards does a brilliant job of explaining a viewfinder.

****

Chapter 9: Painting Tools
Intro to Painting

So, now that you've completed a good drawing foundation, it's time for you to move into the wonderful world of paint. Your decision includes watercolor, acrylic or oil. Pastel is sometimes considered a painting medium as well. Whatever you choose, there are pros and cons to each media. Get to know your paint to overcome any of its limitations.

Watercolor is beautiful. It demands excellent drawing skills. Erasing a mistake takes away from the integrity of the paper. Making a mistake in applying the paint requires a great deal of patience to remove the mistake. I am not a patient person. I would not want to sit for an hour dabbing out one error. Water is its medium. There is no odor. The paints are easy to carry. If you are a patient person and are skilled in drawing, this is the medium for you.

Acrylic paint is water-based. It thins with water. It dries quickly. It does have a bit of an odor. I use acrylic as an underpainting for my oils. I establish all my lights and darks with black and white acrylic. Because it dries quickly, it is sometimes difficult to blend. I have students who use acrylic and are extremely happy with the results.

Oil paint now comes oil-based or water-based. For those of you who want to paint with oil, but want to avoid the solvents, odorless or not, you can now purchase water-based oil paints and oil paints made with walnut oil—a natural medium. These oil paints dry slowly like regular oil paints and have the same blending capacity. I have students who use water-based and walnut-based paint. They are happy with the results and produce beautiful paintings.

I prefer my old, tried and true, regular oil paints. I love the color, I love the feel and I love the smell. I have tried other media and am always happy to come back to my oils. There is a richness to regular oil paint I love. If you decide to work in oils I advise you to learn to work clean. Anything with pigment in it should not come in contact with your skin. If you get paint on your hands, clean them immediately. I do a quick wipe with paint thinner, and then I wash my hands with regular soap and water. A nail brush is a handy tool to have.

Since my preference is for oil and acrylic, this section will deal with tools for these media. To make things more organized, I listed the tools in alphabetical order:

Brushes
Canvas
Camera
Cleaning
Easel
Light
Mahl stick
Miscellaneous
Paint thinner and medium
Palette
Rags
Storage

Brushes

It is important to have good brushes. It makes the painting process much smoother. Oil and acrylic brushes have long handles vs. short handles for watercolor. Watercolor is generally done on a flat surface. Short handles work fine for watercolor.

Long handles allow us to paint away from the canvas.

Do not hold the brush like a pencil. Hold your brush loosely toward the middle. The arm is used to paint giving a greater range of motion and ease to the brush. When just the wrist is used the effect is much more controlled, but stiff. Extend your arm so you are about 3 feet away from your canvas (which should be on an easel). Always begin your painting with your largest brushes. I usually start with a brush that is about 1-inch wide. Then, I use smaller and smaller brushes as I get toward the end of the painting. Helen said, "Start with a broom and finish with a needle." In other words—leave the teeny-tiny details until the very last.

Bristles—Coarse vs. Soft

The paint end of your brush holds the bristles. Bristles can be coarse or soft, natural or synthetic.

There are three bristle types of brushes— natural white bristles, natural soft hair bristles and synthetic bristles. Nowadays, some of the synthetic brands are as good as natural bristles.

Coarse, white bristle brushes are used to apply paint to an unpainted canvas and to mass in a first layer of color. Canvas has a "tooth" to it, which means the surface is rough. It eats brushes. The stiffer bristles are made to withstand the rigorous beating they take when applying paint to a rough canvas surface. My bristles do a fine job of applying the first coat of paint. I don't have to worry about damaging them. I also use my coarse, white bristle brushes to apply my acrylic underpainting (see Chapter 11). In my opinion, the best bristles come from the backs of Chinese hogs. My advice is to purchase the stiffest, white bristle brush you can find. If you are new to painting, I suggest starting with number 6, number 8 and number 10, white bristle brushes.

Nylon or sable brushes have a softer, velvety feel when applying paint. After the initial coat of paint has been applied with the coarse, white bristles and the canvas is less likely to eat the brush, I switch to my softer brushes. It's a bit like painting on silk.

The natural brushes, like sable, can be quite expensive. I've been happy with my collection of nylon brushes. Switch to the softer brushes for the remainder of the paint layers. Never use these good brushes to start your painting.

Brush Shapes: Brights, Filberts, Flats and Rounds

There are four shapes of brushes. They are called brights, filberts, flats and rounds. They have their own specialties when painting. Brushes are numbered. The smaller the number, the smaller the brush. Unfortunately, there is no standard numbering between brands. So, it's a good idea to be aware of the width of the brush. Is it 1-inch wide or one-quarter-inch wide? Then, when your teacher says to purchase a number 4 bright, you'll be aware of the size and not dependent on the number. It's good to have a wide assortment. You can never have too many brushes. Usually, the letter or word of the brush shape is written next to the brush number size- "B" for bright, "F" for filbert, "FL" for flat, "R" for round.

Brights

Brights are flat, short-bristle brushes with a square tip. They are used for painting large areas, such as the background and straight lines. They differ from flats in that their bristles are shorter.

They have a nice spring to them when applying paint.

Filberts

Filberts are flat-bristle brushes with a rounded tip. They are excellent for painting round edges and objects.

Flats

Flats are long, flat-bristle brushes with a square tip (long brights). I use flats less and less now preferring brights. There is more give to flats and I prefer the spring of the shorter bristled brights.

Rounds

Rounds have rounded tips. They are used for painting flower petals. I don't use these much either. However, I do have a small, number 4 round I use for details.

Make sure you put enough paint on your brush. My students tend to be skimpy with their paint. Using a good amount of paint is a good way to protect your brushes.

What's the best brand of brushes? I'm sorry to tell you you'll have to discover that for yourself by trial and error. The one tip I can give you is, if your bristles fall out while you are painting—take the brush/brushes back to wherever you bought them and either get a refund or an exchange. I have found it doesn't matter how much you spend on a brush. Bristles fall out if the brush is poorly made. By returning the brush/brushes, you force the manufacturer to stop making a defective product. My students have had problems with well-known brands. So, there is no easy way to choose brushes. If you find a brand you like—stick with it.

Canvas

It is wise to start off with a good-sized canvas, such as a 16-by-20, so you learn to paint with your arm instead of your wrist.

You can buy stretched canvas (canvas stretched to fit on wooden stretcher strips or stretcher bars), panels, wood panels and canvas paper. I like making my own stretched canvas starting with raw canvas, stretching and stapling it onto the wooden stretcher strips and then, applying a coat or two of gesso. Gesso is a ground (background of a painting) I apply to the raw canvas. This allows the canvas to accept my oil or acrylic paint without seeping through the canvas. The gesso can then be sanded, or not, depending upon what texture you want. Stretched canvas comes in cotton duck and linen. Linen is more expensive than cotton. Stretched canvases are easy to carry and can be hung on the wall for viewing before they are framed.

The nice thing about making my own canvases is I can make any size I want. However, I do find I prefer standard sizes: 5-by-7, 8-by-10, 11-by-14, 16-by-20 and 18-by-24. I like to have a range of sizes to match my mood. Some things really do look better on smaller canvases and some fit better on larger ones. The good news is, if your painting doesn't work on one size, you can try it again on another. Been there, done that.

Some artists enjoy painting on wood panels. I remember using Masonite when I was in college. I loved the feel of the surface.

Canvas panels are cardboard panels with a skin of canvas glued on top. The canvas is rigid and does not give like a stretched canvas. I find the panels difficult to handle because the oil paint gets on the edges and then onto my hands. This is a problem if I need to turn or transport my canvas. The panels have to be left on the easel or propped up against something while they dry. Unlike stretched canvas, there is no give to the canvas panels when you apply the paint.

Canvas paper is also available. I don't like it so I don't have anything nice to say about it. I prefer to be able to pick up my canvas via the stretcher bars. And, I like the give of the canvas as I paint. You could use canvas paper for acrylic, but it doesn't stay flat unless you tape it down and I don't see the point. If you want to do some fast sketches with a brush, get a large newsprint pad to practice sketching. It is much cheaper than canvas paper. Because of its size, a newsprint pad is excellent for practicing and warming up before settling down to your canvas.

Camera

I suggest you buy a digital camera. You can get a decent one for a reasonable price. I am not always able to paint on-site so I take pictures. Lots of pictures. Lots of pictures of the same thing. Usually, out of ten or fifteen shots, I get something I want to paint.

Many of my students like to copy work from other artists. This is fine and a really good way to learn. However, you cannot sell a copy of someone else's work, including other paintings, cards, photos and calendars. Once an artist paints a painting or takes a photograph, that work is automatically copyrighted. It doesn't matter if you change the picture. The fact remains you are using someone else's work.

You may not feel like you will sell your paintings at this point, but you may in time and it is legally better to work from your own photos. If you do work from someone else's work, you must give him or her credit and get his or her permission when you display your painting at a show or an exhibit.

Take your own pictures. It is your personality that should be in your painting. Paint or photograph what is interesting to you. If you have permission to paint from a family member's photo that is all well and good. However, I prefer my students take their own photos and work from what their eyes see. It is more interesting to the viewer to see the world through the artist's eye—not through a surrogate's.

And—SHUT OFF THE FLASH!!!! I'm sorry to be so adamant about this, but the flash adds another "sun" to the photo making it appear unreal. Nowadays, digital cameras are able to adjust to use any available light. No flash is needed.

We are accustomed to taking pictures with a flash, or sitting in a photographer's studio with lights everywhere to erase the shadows. This is fine for a photographic portrait, but for painting all these lights make everything become flat and boring. The shadows actually make things more lifelike because they add interest and negative space. You may have to use a tripod to avoid blurry images.

Which brings me to our next subject—shadows. Don't be afraid of the dark. One of the problems many new artists have is they don't make their darks dark enough. Contrast is what makes things look real. Without those beautiful shadows our painting looks flat. Shadows give dimension to our work. Don't be afraid of them. When you are taking photographs, don't take them at midday with full sun; there won't be any nice dramatic shadows.

Many people believe the only way to paint is from something real. It definitely is the best way to learn. If you want to learn how to paint, set up a still life. I set up a still life whenever I can, but I bring my camera with me wherever I go. I love photographing landscapes where my parents live in Vermont. I'm not there long enough to paint and I would have to cart a ton of equipment with me if I did want to paint. I also live in New England where our warmer weather is short and sweet. My winters are spent painting from the lovely photographs I take all year long.

My feeling is, whether I am working from a still life or from a photograph, I am painting. I don't like bugs, I don't like wind and I don't like sitting out in the hot sun. I also don't like people looking over my shoulder, and it's always nice to have a bathroom handy. So I don't feel guilty when I work from my own photographs.

Cleaning

Cleaning your brushes

During the painting session, I start with a large, metal coffee can. Inside the coffee can I place a cat food can with lots of holes punched in its bottom. I turn the can so the holes are facing up. I fill the coffee can with odorless turpentine or mineral spirits to at least cover the cat food can. I can clean my brush by wiping it on the holes in the cat food can. The paint falls through the holes and this keeps my brush away from all the paint sediment that falls to the bottom of my coffee can. It is very important to constantly clean your brush while painting—especially between color changes. You do not need to use one brush for every color. You simply need to make sure your brush has no traces of a previous color. There is nothing worse than applying paint with a dirty brush.

At the end of each class, I pour my used, odorless thinner/Gamsol from my coffee can into a glass jar (glass, not plastic because plastic melts) for storage. When I come back to paint, the paint sediment has settled to the bottom of the jar. This separation leaves clean thinner/Gamsol at the top I can now pour back into my coffee can at my next painting session. This way, I can reuse my thinner.

As of this writing (2016), we have discovered the same coffee can/cat food can idea in little metal pots (purchased on the internet) complete with handle, cleaning basket and rubber sealed cover. Much more attractive and it does the same thing -- allows the paint to separate from the thinner.

After the painting session, clean your brushes with liquid laundry detergent. I use an old, grated cheese container, fill it with about a half-inch of liquid laundry detergent (no water) and put my dirty brushes in through the cap. Once paint gets dried on the bristles it is very hard to get out. It's best to clean your brushes right after you've used them, but sometimes I leave them in the detergent until morning. Swish them around, remove them from the soap and rinse them in warm water (never hot water as it will melt the glue holding the bristles to your brush.) When there is no soap left in the brush, squeeze out the water with your fingers to reshape the bristles. I find this is the best method. I use the same laundry detergent over and over until there is none left in my container. There is no need to empty it every time.

Cleaning paint out of cloth

Lestoil can be used for cleaning oil paint off fabric. Helen recommended this and it is invaluable for getting oil paint out of clothes. I rub some Lestoil into the paint and then rinse it with water. This works best on fresh stains. Once the paint is dry only a miracle can take the paint out.

Easel

Helen informed us the word easel means donkey in Dutch. It truly is a beast of burden. I have a heavy, wooden easel I use at my house that is like the one Helen used. I have inserted hooks and screws and knobs to hold my mirror, a paint scraper, painting apron, color chart, mahl stick and a thermometer to tell me what the temperature is in my cellar where I have classes. Everything is within reach. I have a wooden box in front of my easel to hold my paints and paint thinner. A tray table to my right (I am right-handed) to hold my brushes and a cup of tea. I have a set of plastic drawers to my left that hold unused rags and tubes of paint.

If I go out to a class or outside to paint, I use one of my lighter weight, metal easels. I find these easy to set up quickly. You can find a metal easel for around $40. Do not purchase a cheap, wooden easel. These are often only for display purposes. You want an easel that can take a beating and won't fall apart after you have used it only once. Be wary of easels that are too complicated. My students used to bring their own easels to class and had to set them up each time. Some of their easels had many knobs and latches. This drove them so crazy they went out and purchased a simpler metal model. The

knobs and latches work fine if you can set your
easel up and leave it in one place.

Position your canvas on your easel so your arm
is not reaching up or you are not bending down to
work. Your arm should be straight. You can adjust
your easel to move your canvas up or down so it is
at eye level. The clamp provided with the easel, to
secure the canvas, tends to overlap the front of the
canvas. This leaves a blank spot on the canvas
when you paint. Bring the top of the canvas
forward a bit and tighten the clamp on top of the
canvas edge instead of overlapping it. This will
prevent the blank spot.

Set your easel up so it is straight up and down
and not at an angle. When an easel is at an angle
and you are using an overhead light, the light can
produce a terrible glare at the top of your canvas.
That can be remedied simply by righting the easel
to 90 degrees to deflect the glare. On my heavy,
wooden easel, I can tilt the angle a bit more forward
at the top because the easel is weighted. Most
portable easels have three, skinny legs (two in the
front, one in the back). If you tilt them forward too
much, they fall over. My wooden easel is anchored
on a wooden square frame with wheels. The wheels
lock into place. The base provides enough support
in front and in back of the easel so I can safely tilt
my painting surface toward me.

When you have been painting awhile and are
ready to make a huge investment in a permanent
structure to paint on, the big wooden easels are a
dream. Mine truly is a "donkey."

Light
I remember all the classes I took over the
years—usually life drawing and painting,

sometimes portrait. There were always two lights or more directed on the model. Since we painted the model for three weeks in succession, it was often hard to repeat the lighting. Once I studied with Helen, this way of lighting became totally absurd to me.

If we are to paint and draw things from life, there is one basic and natural concept to remember: In our world we have only one light source—the Sun. The old masters never had to think about this because they only had the Sun to paint by—or candles. There were no switches whereby fifteen suns appeared and removed every blessed shadow from an entire room. The old masters understood shadows made things real and it was the shadows that added depth. It was the darkness that added mystery and soul to their paintings.

Natural light, of course, is the best light by which to paint. The best natural light comes from the north. If you set up a still life in front of a north lit window, the shadows and light will remain the same throughout the day. Anywhere else and the shadows and light will change every few minutes.

This is quite a challenge for painters who like to paint "plein air," or outside. The light you start off with early in the morning drastically changes by noon. Once I was fortunate to paint in someone's garden over a period of days, I learned to set up the shapes and colors, but only observe the light changes. Then, I would decide on a time of day I would like to capture and work like a fiend recording all the shadows in the correct places at my chosen time.

But, I am not always able to paint outside. And I do love the safety and security of my studio so I have to set up something close to nature.

I place my still life inside a cardboard box where it is sheltered from other lights in my studio and shine a bright light, 75 to 100 watts, on it to get deep, rich shadows and color. I direct a 40W bulb at my canvas. If my easel light is casting an unnatural light on my still life I will hang a cloth in such a way that it blocks my easel light and doesn't catch on fire. I do everything in my power to insure I have only one "sun" shining on my still life.

Why such a low wattage for our canvas? When we hang a finished painting, we usually hang it on a wall without light which gives the painting about 40 watts of illumination. So painting under a brighter light will give an incorrect reading on your canvas. Before I was instructed by Helen, I used 100W bulbs. Then, when I would hang my painting, the colors appeared too light and overexposed. By painting by the light of a 40W bulb, you will get a lovely and correct effect when you are ready to display your painting.

Mahl stick

A mahl stick is long stick (about 3 feet) used while painting lines, details or anything for which you need a steady hand. This was one of Helen's favorite tools. She would often use it when she was cutting in a sharp line or adding a small dab of paint. There is nothing worse than aiming for a small area of your painting with a glob of paint and missing. I use an old boom box antenna that can expand or contract. Yardsticks, dowels or any firm stick also make good mahl sticks.

Miscellaneous

Apron

Even my neatest students get paint on themselves sometimes. Make sure you don't wear your best clothes to paint. And make sure you are covered. Use a long cook's apron or a smock or large shirt. Eventually, your apron will look like a work of art!

Magnifying glass

A magnifying glass is helpful when there is a little bit of detail you can't quite see in your photograph.

Music

Play whatever music inspires you. I like music to stay in the background and fill in the silence. I find New Age music to be more amenable to my painting style. I paint with my own rhythms and emotions, not those of the music.

Paint scraper

A paint scraper (you can buy at any hardware store) is valuable for scraping off a nasty bit of paint from your palette. Layers do build up on my palette and my paint scraper brings back the surface. It is important to clean your palette after every painting session.

Palette knife

This painting tool looks like a mini-trowel. Some people use it to paint. I use it to scrape a dried pool of paint from my palette. I prefer a trowel-shaped palette knife (as opposed to one that looks like a butter knife) because I can get the paint off keeping my fingers away from the paint and the palette. A palette knife is also good for mixing color.

Pliers

Sometimes the covers on my paint tubes stick. I have a cheap pair of pliers I use to gently twist them off.

Rug or drop cloth

Paint spatters. Protect your surrounding floor with some kind of mat, rug or cloth.

Taboret

A taboret is a box or a stool used to hold an artist's palette, turpentine, brushes and anything else needed for painting. I use an old kitchen cabinet turned sideways. Its top supports my palette and my can of odorless paint thinner. I placed the cabinet on top of the front rails of my easel where the wheels are attached. I use the inside of the cabinet to store jars and other supplies I need for painting. You can find taborets online, which can be expensive. My old cabinet was free and it works fine.

Tube wringer

I hate wasting paint. It gets more and more expensive every day. I found a heavy-duty metal tube wringer online for about $11. It works great. I purchased a plastic one years ago. It did a nice job on six tubes of paint and then its gears stripped and that was the end of that. This metal one is a dream. It helps me to get every last drop of paint out of a tube. A good investment.

Paint thinner and medium
Paint thinner

Paint thinner is used to clean your brushes between color changes. There are lots of products from which to choose.

You can choose from turpentine, odorless paint thinner, or Gamsol odorless paint thinner. After using regular odorless paint thinner which, by the way, isn't really odorless for the last twenty years, we have now switched to Gamsol - an odorless paint thinner made by Gamblin which is actually odorless. In a closed area, the regular odorless paint thinner or turpentine has been a bit much to bear.

Here I have to add a special note of thanks to Dave Drinon, the artist-in-residence at the Whistler House Museum in Lowell, Massachusetts. My class and I were invited to visit him and take a tour. What an honor! While in his museum studio, I noticed he had his oil paints out and his pot of thinner next to them. I pretty much stuck my face into his pot of paint thinner. No smell!! Dave explained he was using Gamsol odorless paint thinner--a product made by Gamblin (which also makes an odorless varnish--Gamvar). Within a couple of months of our visit, we were all using Gamsol. What a difference!! It's worth every penny, separates and cleans just like the old smelly stuff did. Thank-you, Dave!!

Stay away from the natural thinners hardware stores now sell. The reason is because the paint doesn't separate from the natural thinner like it does from odorless paint thinner/Gamsol. This means I would have to dispose of my used, natural thinner each time I paint. I don't feel that is economical or "green." I reuse my odorless paint thinner/Gamsol a long time. When my jar gets too full of sediment,

I take it to a hazardous waste facility in my town (see cleaning.)

Medium

Medium is a vehicle artists use to thin their paint to make it easier to spread. Oil painters might use linseed oil, walnut oil, or a combination of turpentine, linseed oil and varnish. Watercolor painters, acrylic painters and water-based oil painters use water.

Note: Water-based oils use water instead of turpentine. They dry like oils, but I find them too sticky. Some of my students use them without a problem.

Helen used a mixture of equal parts Damar varnish, linseed oil and turpentine as her medium. I tried using this, but the varnish made my paintings shiny which, in turn, made them impossible to photograph. I dropped the Damar varnish from my mixture and now use linseed oil and Gamsol after I discovered this quote from Helen: "Linseed oil fortifies the paint; turpentine just thins it."

Palette

Always use a medium-toned palette—gray or brown, but never white. I use a thin piece of plywood. Any kind of wood palette will need a coat of linseed oil applied to its surface before you start mixing paint on it the first time. This prevents the oil color from becoming absorbed into the wood. Some of my students prefer a clear Lucite palette. They tell me it is easier to clean. Make sure whatever is under the Lucite palette is not white. We paint onto gray or color; therefore, a white palette won't represent our colors correctly as we mix. We use a brown paper bag under the palette to make it a neutral color. A thick piece of glass also makes a good palette. That is what we used in college with a layer of duct tape around the edges so we wouldn't get cut.

A gray covered plastic palette is now available online. It is less cumbersome than the old palettes and it fits nicely into my freezer.

Put out all your colors (see Chapter 10) around the outer edge of the palette starting with white, then the warm colors followed by the cool colors and finally black. My students often just put out what they think they will need, but it's best to have all colors out so you can experiment if need be. Use the center of the palette for mixing color. Always wipe off the mixing area at the end of each painting session so your mixing area will be free of dried paint. It is not easy to mix on a rough, mucky surface. If you are not diligent in your cleaning, your palette will become an excavation project that will take a sizeable amount of time to clean. You can't mix properly on lumps and bumps of paint.

Paint does dry out on the palette. Depending on the color, some paint will dry in a week, whereas others will stay moist for a month. Instead of adding more color to a dried-up clump, I take a paint scraper, scrape up the old, dried paint and then apply new paint. It is easier for me to clean as I go along.

Rags

Learn to work clean. I use a piece of Turkish towel rather than a big wad of paper towels. I cut a piece about 4-by-8 inches. I fold it in half and place it in the lower right corner (I am right-handed) of my palette. This way it is conveniently close to my can of thinner and helps me avoid drips. Lefties can reverse their set-up. I will use this piece of towel for many paint sessions. I just keep folding it until it is filled with paint.

Do not hold paint rags in your hand while painting. Even though paint is made from less toxic materials than were used in the past, paint is still made with pigment. Handi-wipes are a nice invention to keep in your painting area. Keep your hands clean of paint and then it won't find its way onto your clothes, furniture or woodwork.

When I want to remove paint from my canvas or clean the mixing area of my palette, I use a small piece of old T-shirt. I'm stressing the word "small." A 4-by-4-inch square will do. My students sometimes use long pieces which drag in their paint then onto their clothes, then onto their hands and it's a mess. Small pieces are better and easier to control.

Paint is self-combustible when left exposed outside of a tube or sealed can. This means the paint-filled rags can catch fire if left unattended. When I need to dispose of a paint rag, it goes into a covered metal bin outside my house. Then I put the rag into the trash on trash day. Do NOT dispose of your paint rags in your house.

Storage

Storing your palette

Oil paint on my palette stays fresher longer when I keep it in my freezer. There are plastic paint boxes available for storing a palette. The cover of the paint box has legs on the inside to keep the palette in place so the box can be carried under your arm like a book. The little legs prevent the palette and paint from shifting around.

The small, gray (neutral color) palette box with a cover mentioned earlier doubles as a palette and a palette box. It is lightweight. It has paint wells for individual colors. The center of the box or the cover can be used to mix colors. It cleans up easily and doesn't take up much space in my freezer.

Storing your paint

I find it is easier to locate a tube of paint if cool and warm colors are kept separate. You can use plastic bags, plastic boxes or any manner of organizational tool that works for you.

Storing your painting

If you work at home, you can leave your painting on your easel. If you have a stretched canvas, you can simply hang it on a nail. Make sure the nail head doesn't poke through the canvas. It will make a puck in the canvas that will be difficult to remove. Likewise, if you lean your stretched canvas against something, make sure there is nothing poking into it.

****

Chapter 10: Color
Color

Color can be a painter's best friend or worst
enemy. When it's right, it's beautiful. When it's
wrong, it's a nightmare. There are a million colors
from which to choose. Without some kind of
guidance, it is easy to get lost. This Chapter focuses
on color—some basics as well as my palette of
colors.

The Color Wheel and Opposite Colors

In painting, a little knowledge of the color
wheel is very useful. The color wheel I refer to is
pretty basic. It consists of the three primary colors
(red, blue and yellow) and three secondary colors
(violet, orange and green). Primary colors are first
because all colors are made from them. You cannot
combine two colors to make primaries. The
secondary colors are made by combining two
primaries: violet (red and blue), orange (red and
yellow) and green (yellow and blue).

The eye MUST see all three primaries or it
produces an unease in our bodies. I was unaware of
this as I began my first painting in my friend's
garden in Framingham, Massachusetts. As I was
painting in all the greens I had this sense, in the
back of my head, I needed to add some red. Green
is comprised of blue and yellow. So, yes, I was
missing some red.

After a few days and much work on all the
greens, I decided it was time to add red. I began
slopping red over all my green. To my horror,
everything, all my beautiful green, began to turn
brown. Did this stop me? Of course not. I added
more red. So, I had more brown (see Chapter 12).

It wasn't until I studied with Helen I learned why this happened. Primary red is the opposite color of secondary green. When you combine two opposite colors you get mud, brown, or what I like to call caca color. Primary blue is opposite secondary orange. Primary yellow is opposite secondary violet. If you mix these together, you get mud. My thought to add the red was correct. My body was telling me the color was missing. If I had confined my red to dabs and flowers, I would not have wrecked the whole painting. Fortunately, because it was paint, I was able to correct my errors and move on.

Every class I have ever taken stressed the avoidance of making mud. But it would have helped me a lot if someone had taught me how to make it so I could avoid it. All my students are taught to make mud.

Opposite colors are also considered complementary. If used correctly, they produce beautiful shadows. If you want green to be darker, add its complement, red. If you want purple to be darker, add a dark yellow (Burnt Umber). If you want dark orange to be darker (Burnt Sienna in my palette), add blue.

With the addition of Ivory Black to these mixtures, you can make the most luscious and darkest of shadows.

Palette of Colors
    Here is my basic palette of colors:
    Zinc White
    Cadmium Yellow Light
    Yellow Ochre
    Burnt Umber
    Cadmium Orange

Raw Sienna
Burnt Sienna
Cadmium Red Light
Grumbacher Red
Venetian Red
Indian Red
Alizarin Crimson
Thalo Blue
Thalo Green
Ivory Black

These are my extra colors:
Cadmium Yellow Medium
Dioxazine Purple
Manganese Violet
Sap Green
Thalo Red Rose
Thalo Yellow Green

When I started painting, I never remember any teacher telling me what colors to use. By the time I graduated from college, I owned every tubed color in every brand imaginable. And, yet, with all these colors, I couldn't paint anything real. I had no idea how to mix colors. I did not understand how to look at color and translate that to a painting. I had to learn to see color and understand it before I could mix it and apply it to canvas. Unfortunately, this was something never taught in all the classes I took.

Just prior to studying with Helen, I was working on a painting project in my apartment, in Framingham, Massachusetts. The painting was of an abstract dancer done in shades of blue. I had let the painting dry and then wanted to go back and work on it. I owned every shade of blue there was—Prussian Blue, Cerulean Blue, Ultramarine

Blue, Cobalt Blue, and Manganese Blue. I didn't use Thalo Blue because I was afraid of it. I tried to remake the original color. I tried every tube of blue, every combination of blue and every mixture of blue. I never was able to reproduce the original color, and in a complete sense of defeat I repainted the entire painting. Painting was always like this for me when using color. I had no clue where to start.

Often my students will ask me, why I use the colors I do. In 1993, when I started studying with Helen, I decided to only use the colors she suggested. Helen's palette consisted of fifteen basic colors. She was the first teacher I ever had who published her palette of colors. I can remember, as I started to apply her principles, how excited I was because, after all these years, I could actually paint an apple, a carrot, a book, hair, water, sand—everything. This palette allowed me to discover, for the first time in my life, the magic of making things look real. From her palette, I can make any color I want. This palette makes clean, beautiful color. Every color works with every other color on the palette without making mud—the painter's worst enemy. Everyone always talks about working with a limited palette. My palette is limited—to these fifteen colors (plus a few extra Helen suggested) and I love the results.

Here is more information on the palette:

Warm Colors

Yellow

Cadmium Yellow Light—a light-toned, bright-intensity yellow.

Yellow Ochre—a medium-toned, medium-intensity yellow.

Burnt Umber—a dark-toned, dull-intensity yellow.

Note: Cadmium Yellow Medium is a nice, extra color. I use it a lot in landscapes and flowers.

Orange (the hottest warm)

Cadmium Orange—a bright-toned, bright-intensity orange.

Raw Sienna—a medium-toned, medium-intensity orange.

Burnt Sienna—a dark-toned, dull-intensity orange.

Red (the coolest warm)

Cadmium Red Light—a light-toned, bright-intensity red.

Note: NEVER use Cadmium Red Medium or Cadmium Red Dark. These are outlawed colors in my class. Where Cadmium Red Light makes a beautiful, clean red that mixes predictably with other colors, the medium and dark make colors look muddied and bruised. They may look pretty in the tube, but once you mix them with another color, they become garish. Stay away from them.

Grumbacher Red—a medium-toned, bright-intensity red. (Grumbacher is a brand name. Each company has its version of this red.)

Venetian Red—a medium-toned, medium-intensity red. Also called, Light Red and Terra Rosa.

Indian Red—a dark-toned, dull-intensity red.

Cool Colors
Violet

Alizarin Crimson

Note: This can, on occasion, be used as a red. Helen advised us any violet or purple would be OK. There are so many violets and purples in nature they are difficult to reproduce. I've added Dioxazine Purple to my palette, plus Manganese Violet and Thalo Red Rose, two of Helen's extra colors.

Blue

Thalo Blue (also spelled Pthalo Blue and Pthalocyanine Blue)

Note: Many people tend to stay away from Thalo Blue because of its intensity. Helen used only Thalo Blue. She taught us if we needed a bright, lively blue, there was no other blue that could give us the brightness. And, by mixing Thalo Blue with the other colors of our palette, we could reproduce all other blues. Even though I was fearful of Thalo Blue at first, I came to understand how to use it and mix it with other colors. Since 1993, I have never needed any other blue, and I have never had a recurrence of my impossible to mix blue story!

Helen, in her book My Thirteen Colors, provides the recipes for mixing Thalo Blue to make Cerulean, Cobalt, Ultramarine and Manganese Blue.

Green

Thalo Green (also spelled Pthalo Green and Pthalocyanine Green)

Note: Here again the intensity of this color can be quite frightening, but mixed with other colors, it is a magnificent addition to your palette.

When you have tried every mixture possible attempting to make a particular green, try using Thalo Blue instead. Mixed with the yellow or orange of this palette, it makes a delicious green and can produce any green you see in nature. Also, a combination of yellow and Ivory Black makes an interesting mixture of green.

White and Black

White and black are NOT colors. They are used to darken and lighten colors and to make gray. They look lifeless and dead next to colors. So, always add some color to a mixture of black and white. Do not use black alone. Do not use white alone. Always add color. Sorry to be redundant, but I say this at least once a week in my classes.

White

Zinc White (a warm white). I use this because of its warmth.

Titanium White

Black

Ivory Black

Note: Until I studied with Helen I was told never to use black. She used a lovely, transparent black to make the most beautiful grays. Because it is transparent, this black does not dull or muddy the colors with which it mixes. By adding Ivory Black, I have found my mixtures of colors are more varied, richer and more natural looking.

Extra Colors

Cadmium Yellow Medium—a delicious, orangey yellow I love to use for sunflowers.

Dioxazine Purple

Note: this was a color my students found. This is a purple with which we have had much success.

Manganese Violet—not available in all paint brands, but a lovely violet.

Sap Green—a nice addition to a palette, especially if you do a lot of landscapes. Helen often used this tubed Sap Green in her paintings. You can make Sap Green by using Thalo Green, Yellow Ochre and Ivory Black—because of the opaqueness of the Yellow Ochre, it makes an opaque color, which is great for coverage. Tubed Sap Green is very transparent and great to use as a glaze.

Thalo Red Rose—a reddish violet.

Thalo Yellow Green—a bright yellow-green. Excellent for landscapes.

Mixing Color

It is easier to darken a color than it is to lighten one. Start with the lightest color first and then add the darker color. This is easily and quickly done. If you start with a dark color and try to lighten it, you will end up with a pile of paint that doesn't turn lighter. This I know from experience.

****

Chapter 11: Techniques and Tips
Brushstrokes

There are two ways to use your brush (this is for flats, brights and filberts). You can use the whole brush or you can use just the edge. For some reason, I keep finding my students using only the edges of their brushes to apply paint. This gives the painting a look I call chicken scratches. Instead of a nice flat stroke that applies paint to the canvas in a wide swath, I find them scratching the paint on with the edge. Would you paint a house using just the edge of the brush? No, you would use the whole body of the brush to get better coverage.

I watch my students apply paint in 12-inch strokes either vertically or horizontally. Your brushstrokes should never be longer than 1-and-a-half inches. Anything longer and you are painting a house. Learn to vary the direction of your brushstrokes.

Brushstrokes should never go all in the same direction. It is automatic for us to do this, but not what a painting needs. You are NOT painting a house. These kinds of strokes make the painting look flat and boring. Be aware when you start doing something automatically.

Composition

What is composition? That is always a hard question to answer. It is about placement of shapes on your canvas or paper. Nonobjective or abstract art also has composition. The eye should not be led off the canvas. A nicely placed composition allows the eye to move around the artwork and enjoy the view without falling off the edge. As I tell my students, if your composition is lousy, but your drawing is absolutely perfect—then your drawing goes into the trash. If your composition is perfect, but your drawing is not as good—you might be able to sell it. Composition is extremely important.

We are taught in school to put everything into the center of the page ignoring the space around the edges. This works great for a term paper or report, but is truly uninteresting in a painting or drawing. Make your shapes interesting—this includes the spaces.

Compose your picture with an eye for interesting negative shapes (see Chapter 8) including the spaces at the edge of your picture. Make sure objects do not repeat themselves in width or height. A composition is more successful when the main area of the picture is not dead center. A little off to the side is a good choice. An odd number of shapes and spaces is artistically more appealing than even numbers. For example: three or five objects instead of two or four.

I always spend a few hours on placement and composition. I've had paintings that were not quite right in the composition department and they were next to impossible to fix after the painting got started. When my composition is off I can't look at the piece without feeling disturbed. Better to spend the time to find the correct fit for your spaces and shapes before you start developing a painting.

Experiment

Experiment. My students are always asking me what color to use. I suggest a mixture and then say, "Try it." You have to put your mixture next to other colors to see if it will work. If it doesn't work, I try another color or adjust the color I am using.

It's just paint. Color is not an exact science. The world will not end if you don't get it perfect the second you put your brush on the canvas. I wish I could be like Helen and get the color right the first time. But I have to be happy with my third or fourth attempt.

My students want all the answers before they try something. Painting doesn't work that way. There is a certain amount of risk involved. As Helen would say, "You have a fifty-fifty chance—a mess or a masterpiece." Those are pretty amazing odds. Fear is one of the greatest detriments to your painting. It's only paint, a canvas, or another piece of drawing paper you have to replace. The art police aren't going to come and cut off your hands because something doesn't work in your picture.

Try a brushstroke, try a color, a shape, and see what happens. You can always paint over it. Try different subject matter. Experiment with how you look at things. The only thing that can happen is you will learn something. That's a pretty good deal. You may not get how to paint oranges or a face or a rose right away. Instead of feeling like the worst artist in the world Helen would say, "You just have to practice more."

If you have never painted landscapes, because they are new to you, they will be a challenge. The more you paint landscapes, the easier it will become. When I get frustrated with my progress, I remind myself of Helen's words. And I tell myself I am not good at this because I don't know this subject matter well enough so I need to practice more.

Dive into that painting you have always wanted to do. Experiment. Play. Let it teach you.

Get Away from the Canvas (or Drawing)

When we sit on top of our work, we can't really see it. It is always a good idea to step back from the drawing or painting every ten or twenty minutes to actually see the artwork. We get so mired in a little corner of our painting we can't see the bigger picture and how it relates to the whole. And yet, my students will sit up close to their work as if they are chained to it. As soon as I pry them away from their painting they all say the same thing— "Oh! It doesn't look so bad back here!!" Paintings are not looked at from 6 inches away. They are viewed from 6 feet or more.

I get away from my canvas in order to see the color and the shapes. Things pop out at me saying, "Fix me!" If I am working from one of my photos and am struggling with some part of the painting, I turn the painting and photo upside down, walk away and use my mirror. It really does help.

Glazes and Layers of Paint

An oil painting needs layers. It looks starved when it doesn't have enough paint. The addition of layers adds depth and color.

I always start with an acrylic underpainting in black and white. This is an excellent backdrop for the colors (See Chapter 12).

My first layer of oil is mostly medium (odorless turpentine) with a little bit of color added in. This is called a glaze. It allows the underpainting to show through. A glaze is used to add color and/or tone without destroying the brushwork underneath. The glazing paint must be transparent (not opaque). The area where the glaze is applied must be dry. Thin layers dry faster than thick so it is always wise to start thin. Try to avoid adding white at this stage as it dries slowly.

I experiment with my colors in this first layer. I try to get it "in the ballpark" knowing I will be going back and adding more color later. Each layer gets thicker and thicker until I am finished with my painting. I cover my entire canvas with this first layer. Then I cover my entire canvas with a second, thicker layer of paint. This requires me to work quickly adding my impressions of my subject matter. This is not the time to be bogged down in how perfect things should be. That comes at the very end. Now is the time to play, experiment and become familiar with your painting.

As you add layers of color, try not to mix your colors to death. Overmixing flattens the color and takes the life out of it. Sometimes I mix on my palette and sometimes I mix paint into color already on my canvas. I use my brush to mix.

Kisses

Now I know everyone knows what a kiss is: It is the sweet moment when lips meet. But in painting a kiss is where two lines meet, or two angles or an angle and a line. For example, in your painting, if you have a house with a peak on it and a tree intersects that peak—that is a kiss. If you are painting two oranges (or an orange and an apple) and the two pieces of fruit are touching each other's side—that is a kiss. Kisses destroy dimension and our challenge as artists is to make something look three-dimensional on a two-dimensional surface. You must not "kiss on canvas."

To rectify the kiss on the house, you could move the tree a little to the left or right of the peak so it is no longer intersecting. With the fruit, you could place one behind the other so they are no longer kissing. Placing the objects behind and in front of one another creates a feeling of space.

This was one of those lessons I never learned in all the years I took drawing and painting. It is such a simple little thing and makes such a profound difference in an artwork I am surprised it was never taught. During the summer I studied with Helen, she covered the subject of kissing. She devoted an entire class to it and it really hit home. I was working on a complicated still life which included striped wallpaper, a candle, a stack of books, a glass of wine and a crocheted doily on a round table.

I brought my painting into the class I was teaching and presented it to my students. My classes were small so I usually painted along with the class. I told them what I had learned about kisses at my Friday class with Helen. They promptly began to find kisses everywhere in my painting. As I recall there were sixteen. The stripes in the wallpaper were intersecting with the book edges and the candle, the book edges were kissing each other, the round doily was kissing the edge of the round table, the wine glass base was kissing the edge of the doily—it was a mess. In order to fix all these kisses, I had to make miniscule adjustments to my painting—a quarter of an inch there, a 16th of an inch here, until all the kisses were fixed. It worked out to be a great class for my students and for me. It also made a tremendous difference in my painting. We could all see how removing the kisses made the painting feel more three-dimensional.

Let Go

Artists tend to fall in love with their work while they are working on it. An artist must always be aware this clouds his or her judgment of the artwork. It's like a romance. We fall in love with the beloved and cannot see him or her clearly. Detachment is a hard lesson for artists to learn, but without detachment, the artwork can become strangled as we try to hold it to our ideal. My feeling has always been that once you create something, it then develops a life of its own much like children do.

In many art schools there is a practice used to help the student let go of his or her expectations. I've not seen this practice done, but I have heard about it. As one teacher relayed to me, he had a student, who was much in love with his painting. So much so, this student could no longer let go of what he had already done and could no longer view his artwork objectively. His mind was strangling his work. So, the teacher went up to the student's beloved canvas and, with a knife, slashed it through the center. There is no repair method for a torn canvas.

Every time this story comes to mind the air is simply sucked out of my lungs. While the method is violent the point is important. If you can't let go, you can't paint. As Helen would say, "If you can't change, don't paint." Drawing and painting are about change. From beginning to end the artist is correcting what went before in order that the painting may survive as a whole. If you have designated an area of your painting as sacred space—the painting is doomed. You must be able to move all things to benefit the painting.

Squint Your Eyes

Yes, I did say that. It sounds bizarre, but by squinting your eyes, you are actually able to see the lights and darks pop out. I need all the help I can get and this one is free. Squinting eliminates all the unnecessary details and helps you to see the bigger masses. It is especially helpful when you are not sure about your shadows.

****

Chapter 12: The Process
Still Life, Landscape or Portrait?

You have decided to paint. If you are not taking a class and want to work on your own, here are some thoughts about what to paint and how to proceed.

Still Life

Helen would often say, "If you want to learn how to paint, set up a still life." This is the best way to learn to work with light and shapes. It gives you time to study your subject at your own convenience. Find a quite place to work and shut off your cell phone. Set up a still life using an odd number of pieces. Odd numbers are always more interesting. Try not to place the main object dead center on your canvas. Remember we only have one light source in the world—our Sun. So buy one of those clip-on lamps and make sure you have only one light source for your still life. If you have more than one shadow, you have more than one light source.

Helen would place her still life in a cut up cardboard box. I have adopted this practice as it eliminates other light sources from windows and classroom lighting. Direct a strong light onto your still life. A 100W light bulb is a good choice. Play with the lighting until you have shadows you like (See Chapter 9).

Make sure your objects are not all the same height. Vary their textures. Place some in front of others. There should not be blank space around each and every object.

Landscape

In my first years of ignorance as an artist, I arrogantly thought I would like to go out and paint like Monet. What I had failed to realize was Monet painted every day. He studied his art every day. He experimented every day. But, Monet, too, had to start somewhere.

So I decided to set up my paints in the elaborate garden of a friend. When I say garden it wasn't your tomato and cucumber variety of garden. This had terraces and stone pillars, walkways and every species of plant life known in the state of Massachusetts. As I am now older and, hopefully, wiser, I am utterly amazed at what I thought I could accomplish with my limited experience. This is on the level of expecting to fly when you jump out of an airplane instead of using a parachute.

My friend gave me his OK to paint in his garden and I eagerly packed up my red Toyota Tercel with everything I might possibly need on my painting adventure. It took me about an hour to unload the car. The romance was starting to sour a bit, but I cheerfully continued with my set up. The easel, canvas (of course, it was huge! All the better to fly away in a big wind!), palette, paints, turpentine, rags, something to drink, pliers, and on and on until I had created a little outdoor room for myself.

I was finally ready to begin. I quickly placed the major components to make a good composition. I could hear the drumroll as I picked up my brush to begin applying color. Then, I heard my mouth utter, "Oh, my God!! It's all green!!" This statement could only have been made by someone who lived in an apartment. My lack of awareness was rather astonishing. Little lights started popping in my head. I was going to have to figure all this out. What was I thinking?

Luckily, artists are problem-solvers. Unfortunately, at this stage of my education, I did not have a good working knowledge of color and having many tubes of green did not help me to understand how to paint all the green things in the garden. But ignorance is bliss and I trudged onward hoping some light from above would appear and grant me knowledge.

No such luck. I began mixing colors to the best of my ability. After three or four tries I found the colors I needed. But everything was still green. How would I make the different plants stand out? How could I paint them to look different from every other green thing in front of me? Then some light dawned, hallelujah. I saw the greens were not the same. Some were dark, some were light. Then, I started to apply shape personalities to the individual plants—some were pointy, some were shaped like balls, some were messy, some were soft, some were scratchy, some were droopy, and some were rigid. Eventually, I was able to do a plant portrait of each one. It was a monumental exercise in "seeing."

I returned to the garden a few more times. I got better at packing and setting up. The space became more and more familiar and I started to relax as I pretended to be Monet. The painting progressed. I learned a lot. There were some hiccups, but I survived them. There was one last tree to put in the painting, but I debated adding the tree because it was dying. I imagined its personality like I had been doing with all the other plants.

Up till now, I could only see the tree as dying. It had not seemed interesting to paint. But then, as I started to capture its "portrait" I found a new awareness of this plant creature. The tree was not a giant sentinel of a tree, it was one planted for its flowers and fruit. It was about 15 feet tall and many branches grew from its narrow trunk. Its arms were held upward as if it was praying to the Sun and I could feel that, in its dying, its stance was regal and proud. It reached with grace and beauty even though I could see the exhaustion in its reaching. It was proud in death. Proud it was chosen for this special spot in this old, established garden. I had to paint its death because there was so much beauty and dignity in it.

From then on, whenever I walked, I would look at the trees along my path and imagine what personalities they had. Some made me laugh. Some didn't care. Some I could see were aloof and rigid. And some were downright tough.

Without empathy, an artist is lost. We must feel, or try to feel, how each creature we paint has come to this life. Without the ability to reach out to our subject, the subject remains lifeless and dull.

Portrait

If you like a challenge and you have a great deal of patience or want to learn to have patience, try doing a portrait. I recommend not doing family members because they often trigger unwanted psychological traumas while we are painting. It's much easier to paint someone you don't know personally.

Portraits are not about the subject's features. Features actually only occupy one quarter of the entire skull. Yet they are the first things students want to paint—myself included. After years of struggling to find the answers, I started to notice the features on my portraits did not respond well to two or three hours of constant feature adjusting. I would change and move and change and move and the likeness would not quite come. I spent eight hours one day on a portrait I was doing for some friends. I was so frustrated I finally gave up and called it a day. I moved every feature at least ten times with no success.

With a fresh start the next day, I realized the skull was wrong. Once I fixed that—the portrait was finished.

How Do I Start?

How do I start? I have been asked this question more times than I care to remember. I start with a still life or a picture I love. Then I sketch my subject matter onto my canvas with a large bristle brush dipped in black acrylic paint. This is the composition and the most important part of the picture. This is where I spend the most time— getting it on the canvas (see Chapter 11). When I am satisfied with my sketch I then add my darks and lights. In painting, it's not just the shapes that make up the composition; it is also the values—the darks and the lights.

Now that you've had your basic class in drawing, you are ready to paint. Just to clarify, we are using oil and acrylic paint. Here is the general procedure I use:

1. Sketch in black acrylic with a brush.
2. Add the lights and darks in acrylic.
3. Add oil paint color—a thin glaze.
4. Add thicker oil paint—large shapes only.
5. Add thicker oil paint—medium shapes only.
6. Add the details.

It really is a tad more complicated, but this is a good place to start.

When I first studied with Helen, I had a terrible time painting in black and white. I had never been trained to see values (see Chapter 8). But, because this is what Helen did—it is what I did. We don't think of objects as dark or light. We think of an apple as red, a banana as yellow. If we paint what we think, we end up with flat, cartoonish paintings. Red is dark, light and a million shades in between. An apple against a dark background is light, but against a light background it is dark. Helen painted these value paintings for the first eight years of her career. She could see light and dark like Superman could see with his X-ray vision.

Many years down the road, I decided to skip the underpainting step. I went straight to the white canvas. I painted, and painted and painted. I added more and more paint. I couldn't remember when I had last worked so hard to cover a canvas. The struggle went on, layer after layer. Then, a little lightbulb went on in my head. Ah!!!! I hadn't done an underpainting this time. Guess what? I haven't missed this step since. It really does make the process easier.

Helen used her old brushes for acrylic. I do the same. My strong bristles are better suited to handle the roughness of my canvas in the initial stages. Some of my brights are now filberts and some of my flats are now brights. I would never think to use my finer brushes on a raw canvas.

I find Mars Black and Titanium White acrylic work best for the underpainting. They dry fast. Why black? Helen would tell us she started with black so she could see her mistakes better. I can make quick changes with acrylic and the Mars Black makes an excellent dark. Note: DO NOT USE THIS BLACK TO MIX COLOR. It is too strong and will annihilate your colors. This is just for underpainting.

Work with your largest brushes and the largest shapes first—and I mean the largest. Large brushes keep you from getting all caught up in the details. Details are for the end. When you start with the details, you spend the rest of the painting trying to paint around them. This makes the painting process rigid. Your big shapes of dark and light must be correct, or your details will be meaningless. Switch to your medium-sized and smaller-sized brushes as you move through the painting process to the medium-sized and smaller-sized shapes. And don't forget to keep your brushstrokes no longer than 1 to 1-and-a-half inches.

The Middle—Adding Color

I find using an underpainting really simplifies the painting process for me. When I finally start to add color (usually at my second or third sitting) I am already acquainted with my subject matter—its good points and challenges.

Put ALL your colors out. I see some of my students put out three, skimpy, little colors and then expect to paint with them. What if you need more dark? What if you feel some blue would be helpful? If all the colors are not there to choose from, it is easier to ignore that urge for a little more blue. A limited palette stifles your color application. Yes, some people like to paint with a limited palette. I like more choices. And, as I mentioned earlier, this is the best collection of colors I have ever used. I want them all at hand.

It is a good idea to put a thin coat of color (a glaze) on the first layer. Apply the faster drying colors first. The lighter colors dry much slower, which may result in the paint cracking down the road. Use your darker colors as glazes. A glaze is a small amount of paint mixed with your medium and applied to the canvas. I use a glaze of Raw Sienna to start my color. A skinny layer of paint gives the consecutive layers something to hold on to. I find Raw Sienna to be fairly neutral and it gives a lovely glow to everything. Sometimes I glaze in individual colors, but lately, I've been covering the entire canvas with just Raw Sienna. Then I add more colors to the next layer.

Work the whole painting at once. Don't just paint in one little corner. The painting needs to develop as a whole. Helen worked quickly often finishing a painting in one sitting. I tend to "study" my subject matter over time. I work a little here. I work a little there. If I am putting on a second or third layer of paint, the layer is completed on the whole canvas before the sitting is over. There will not be corners starving for paint as my painting progresses.

Do I get the color right on the first try? Do I get the shape in the right place on the first or second try? Do I get my darks dark enough at this stage? The answer to each of these questions is a resounding "NO!" Every stage, every color, every placement, is an experiment. So, if something doesn't materialize immediately to your liking let it go. Work on another area of the canvas. Develop it a little. Let it go and move on.

At this stage, my painting has a bit of a dreamy feel. Nothing is in focus. There are no eyes if this is a portrait, no straight lines if this is perspective, no individual grapes if this is a still life. My subject matter has a vagueness to it as I search to find the color and place the shapes. This middle stage could go on for a while. I spend the most time here. For me, the middle stage requires three, maybe four complete layers of paint. Paint looks better when there is more of it on the canvas. Layers add a richness and depth one layer can't achieve. When I look at nature I see everything is composed of layers—the layers of flesh and bone that make up a hand, layers of leaves that make up a tree, and layers of vegetation in a field or even a lawn. So, if nature is made up of layers, and we are trying to emulate nature's layers, then layers of paint are essential.

Final Stage

As we get closer to the completion of the painting, it is important to use your mirror often and get away from the canvas as much as possible. So many times I see students glued to their canvases. They are not seeing what they are doing. They are so obsessed with the inch they are working on they don't see how it is affecting the rest of the painting. This may be the time to apply some glazes.

This is when I spend more time looking at my painting and less time painting it. What is it saying to me? Are there any glaring issues? Do colors stand out that shouldn't? Are there shapes that don't add to the picture? Is there a detail that needs to be added?

Ah yes, the details. Now it is time to add them. The first things you see in a painting are the last things painted. This is a good time to use smaller brushes. When the final strokes are placed and you are satisfied with the result, it is time to sign the painting. I use my smallest brush and I sign quickly. If I spend too much time trying to make my signature perfect, I end up wrecking my picture. This event should not be the most traumatic of the painting process. Load up your brush (several times if you need to) and sign away.

You can use your initials or an initial and a last name. I once had a student sign his painting as Vincent Monet. I believe his name was Gary. I suggest using your own name.

An oil painting can take up to six months to completely dry. Once the painting is dry, it is a good idea to apply a protective layer of varnish. Helen used Damar varnish. It can be sprayed on or applied with a rag. Do not use a brush because it leaves brushstrokes.

I highly recommend photographing your finished work before it is varnished. I wish I had photos of my earliest paintings. This is a good way to watch your progress and keep a record if you should sell your painting.

Frame It

There is nothing so uplifting to a painting and the painter then adding a lovely frame. The frame should not be chosen to match your wallpaper. It should be chosen to show your painting in its best light. I always attach a label to the back with the painting's title, dimensions, medium (for example, oil on canvas) and price or NFS (not for sale). This makes it easier to keep track of your work. If you become brave enough to enter your work in a local art show through one of the art societies or leagues in your area, it is a good idea to have a photograph and written information describing your art.

Hang it up. There is nothing so self-defeating and detrimental to your painting progress than to tuck your work behind a dresser or leave it in the trunk of your car. The part of your brain that painted this painting is being told you don't

152

appreciate your effort. Hang it up! Respect your work and yourself. HANG IT UP!

Attitude

At some point during the process of painting many of my students start beating themselves up. They say things like: The color isn't right; the line is in the wrong place, something is too light, the subject matter doesn't look right; I'm screwing this all up, and so on. Well, yeah!!!! This isn't the end of the painting. It's just the first stages. Don't judge your painting while you are painting it. Let it develop on its own. Helen's advice to us was, "Painting is a series of corrections." It's not a series of getting everything right on the first try.

I wish I had Helen's gift and experience, but I don't. I might get the color on the third try, but I know I will get it eventually. What's great about this is I have a lovely couple of layers shining underneath making my color richer and deeper. There is no failure—it is simply part of the learning process. If I beat myself up because I have missed perfection, I make an environment where I don't want to paint anymore. Just paint. Don't judge.

If this is the beginning of the painting say, "This is a good start." Not "Oh, my God, this isn't good enough to hang in the Museum of Fine Arts." Geez! No pressure here. Be happy with where you are at—not where you are going. During one of Helen's classes someone asked her how she managed to always paint so well. In typical Helen fashion she answered, "I don't expect too much."

This is a profound truth we all need to accept. This was from Helen, the goddess of painting. I've watched too many students rake themselves over the coals because they don't measure up to some unseen standard. When students decide they are awful there is no way to pull them out of the hole they have put themselves in. You can't find all the answers in the first hour of painting. I discover answers right up to the point of signing my painting (and sometimes way after).

How fast and how far you progress depends on your skill level, the amount of time you are able to spend each week on painting and how much you are able to practice. If you have never painted sheep before—sheep will be a challenge. You have to present your right brain with problems to solve. It functions well in the background and, voila, it comes up with the answers. Maybe not right away, but eventually. Present the problem and then be content to wait while you paint. If you can only paint a few weeks out of year, do not expect to be Monet or Rembrandt.

When I first studied with Helen, I was trying everything she suggested. I would get so frustrated and upset that I wasn't as good as she was. One day, that little, wise voice in my head said, "But I'm not Helen." I can't be Helen. I can only be me. Helen would say, "When you've painted for fifty years, you will be this good, too." And then she would say, "If you don't paint flowers (or rocks or oranges) well, it just means you need to practice more." The more I forgive myself for not being perfect the better I paint.

As we would watch Helen each Friday morning in Rockport, we would all be shaking our heads at her lack of fear when she painted. We were all riddled with fear. She turned from her canvas and said, "What is the worst that could happen?" It never occurred to us to simply start another painting on another canvas. If it doesn't work—start over!

We think we must get the subject perfect on our first try. Paint one apple and that's it? Never paint another apple again? How many haystacks did Monet paint? How many versions of a church did he paint, trying to capture the light at half hour intervals? Think of the piano analogy again. If you want to perfect a piece by Beethoven—you'll need to play it a few times. You'll need to practice in order to get it right.

Of course, I have to add my own story here. In my attempt to paint the luscious garden in Framingham, Massachusetts, I had managed to complete one painting and start another. This second one was really turning out well. I had finally mastered some of the green and I loved the composition. I was using a long, narrow canvas. There was a house in the distant background. A path led from the house to a brick wall with a mailbox built into it.

I was afraid of the bricks, but I couldn't put off painting them any longer. I completed the challenge after a couple of hours. It was perfect. I had done a beautiful rendition of the wall with the mailbox, but then it dawned on me the mailbox was in the wrong place. My next choice was to hyperventilate or hold my breath in shock. I would have to move it if I wanted it right. And I wanted it right. Maybe, since I had painted this perfectly already I could paint it perfectly again? When I resumed breathing, I moved the mailbox. It was perfect!

However, it was still not quite in the right place. This time I didn't stop breathing. I just moved the damn thing. Took me about fifteen minutes. Less emotion, easier to move. As Helen would say, "If you can't change, don't paint."

It's paint. It can be changed, painted again, added to, and removed. Be involved in the process—not the product. Don't pick out your frame and decide where you are going to hang your painting before it's finished. Don't put your creativity inside a framework and rigidly try to force your painting to fit into your expectations. Let your painting develop. It will eventually tell you what it needs.

You can't get to the top of Mount Everest without climbing the mountain. Don't be in a big hurry to get to the top because all you will have do is climb back down and start over.

The Jamaican Model

Everything I teach comes from my own experience. This was a particularly powerful ah ha moment in my painting career.

When I was taking classes at the De Cordova, we were visited by the most gorgeous, exotic man I had ever seen. He had a cloud of dreadlocks tousled around his head, and he was a remarkable shade of chestnut.

He took his pose on the model stand. I was now going to paint the most glorious painting of this heavenly creature. Did I mention he was naked? I dove in to my painting with a passion and fury I had not remembered experiencing before. We had three weeks (three, three-hour sessions) to complete the painting. It is entirely possible I forgot to breathe. I was determined to make the painting magnificent. My expectations were high.

Unfortunately, I did not have the skill level, the knowledge of color, or the palette I have now to paint this man's portrait. To make matters worse, he didn't bother to put on a robe when he took breaks.

He would wander around, totally naked, looking at our work. I am so surprised I didn't faint or melt into a puddle when he came to gaze at my painting. I may have hyperventilated a little. Just imagining him standing next to me takes my breath away thirty years later.

Sadly, in my painting, I made him look ugly. And green. I didn't have a tube of chestnut paint. I couldn't match his skin color. I couldn't capture his pose. The more beautiful I tried to paint him, the uglier he got. It was humiliating. I was devastated. It was a downhill slide for three weeks. In a panic I tried to save what I had done. Nothing worked. It was as if something had died inside of me.

But, I had paid for my semester, which meant very humbled and licking my wounds, I had to return to paint again. We had a new model. I began my painting. Perhaps it was during the second week I noticed my brush was actually capturing what I was looking at. It was as if someone else was controlling my painting hand. Magic? Was I possessed? How could I be doing this when my last attempt had been such a horrific experience?

I'm not sure when my epiphany happened, but some part of me understood I could paint this model because of all the problems I had painting the Jamaican god. At that moment I realized my profound struggle simply meant I was learning—not failing, as I had interpreted my previous situation. From the ashes rose a newfound confidence, a new understanding. I could figure something out—eventually. I was released from the need for perfection.

The Jamaican model returned to our class two more times. Did I paint him magnificently? Yes, I did, and I sold both paintings. The moral of the story: There are no mistakes—only lessons.

****

Final Thoughts

There was never an artist as charming, knowledgeable and entertaining as Helen Van Wyk. The students who studied with her for more than twenty-five years are to be envied. Many artists cannot teach and many teachers cannot teach basic principles. Helen was an artist and a teacher, who could do both.

Helen came out with a group of videos of her "Welcome to My Studio" programs filmed for PBS. There were eleven seasons, each with ten, thirty-minute segments. Every weekend, I still watch Helen's videos. It brings me right back to Rockport, Massachusetts, in 1993. It is now almost twenty years later as I am writing this. Helen will forever be my teacher. As I watch the videos and listen to Helen, she fills me with inspiration, she charms me with her expressive style of teaching and she makes me laugh. She was so proficient with her paint and her color. Even though I have seen each episode many times, I still take notes and try to remember what Helen is saying.

While 1993 was not the ultimate time technology-wise, it was a time when programs were saved for posterity. Having Helen's videos brings her wisdom to my fingertips. Helen taped her shows for WMHT, a PBS station in Plattsburgh, New York. At this writing, it is still possible to find Helen's videos on its website (http://www.wmht.org).

Helen also wrote a series of books. Many are now out-of-print. However, if you can find them, they are well worth adding to your library. Here is a list of Helen's books:

Acrylic Portrait Painting
Basic Oil Painting the Van Wyk Way

Casselwyk Book on Oil Painting
Color Mixing in Action
Color Mixing the Van Wyk Way (Color
Mixing in Action and My 13 Colors)
My 13 Colors and How to Use Them
Painting Flowers the Van Wyk Way
Portraits in Oil the Van Wyk Way
Successful Color Mixtures
Welcome to My Studio
Welcome to My Studio (new revised edition)
Your Painting Questions Answered A to Z

When I took classes from Helen, I would go
home after class and try to apply what she had
taught us. I figured I had nothing to lose by trying
because I couldn't paint. Helen knew more than me.
She had more knowledge, experience and wisdom.
I was determined to absorb every bit of knowledge I
could from her. Here was a teacher who was
actually teaching me how to use paint after all these
years. I adopted her methods, her principles and her
colors way back when. I have never been sorry.
Not only do these principles work for me, they work
for my students.

Helen is in every class I teach. My students
will often hear me say, "Helen says," as I explain
another principle to them. When one student asked
me why I always talked about Helen, my answer
was, Helen is the reason I can paint. She is the
reason I can teach painting. And now she is the
reason I am writing. Of course, my own experience
and words of wisdom get thrown into the mix, but
Helen's principles give me a foundation on which to
base my thoughts. She is, and always will be, my
authority on painting. If Helen said it—it is law.

Helen, wherever you are, I hope I have provided a means to continue your name and principles. You will always be the image I aspire to as artist, teacher and writer.

To the reader of this book, thank-you for coming along on this journey through my personal art history. I hope it has provided you with insight and encouragement to follow your own art journey. Remember—no talent required!

Since this book started with Helen, let's finish with a couple more Helenisms. One of my favorites is, "You've got to do it wrong before you can do it right." As Helen was completing one of her paintings during one of the last times I saw her in Rockport, she suddenly turned around to face us and said, "I'm the only one getting better here!!" In other words—go create, go draw and go paint!

The End

****

About the Author

Kathleen E. Hebert (Kathy) is an artist, art instructor and now author with her first book, *No Talent Required: from Paint by Numbers to Art Instructor*. She lives with her two cats, Lucy and Coal, painting, teaching, writing, gardening and sometimes belly dancing in Worcester, Massachusetts. You can see her artwork and her students' artwork on her self-built website http://kathleenhebertartist.com/. She loves teaching adults how to draw and paint and looks forward to many more exciting art adventures.

Connect with Me:
Follow me on Twitter:
http://twitter.com/artkat2011
Friend me on Facebook:
http://facebook.com/kathleenartkathebert/
Subscribe to my blog:
http://kathleenhebertartist.com/blogger.html
Favorite me at Smashwords:
http://smashwords.com/profile/view/artkat